WITHDRAWN

 S0-BRD-844

Mutual
and Balanced
Force

DATE DUE			
Dec 11 '81			

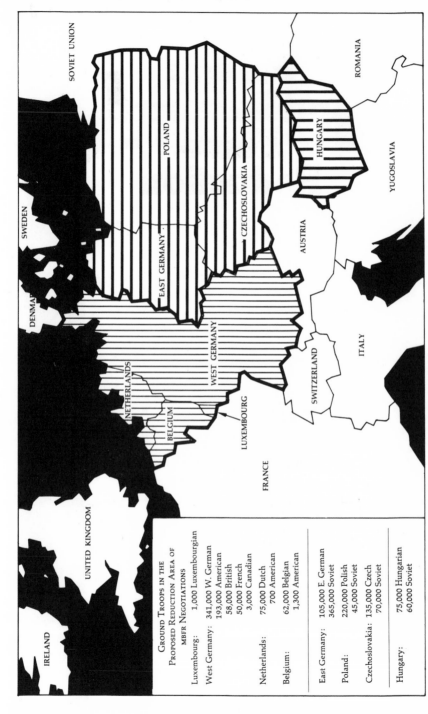

Ground Troops in the Proposed Reduction Area of mbfr Negotiations

Luxembourg:	1,000 Luxembourgian
West Germany:	341,000 W. German
	193,000 American
	58,000 British
	50,000 French
	3,000 Canadian
Netherlands:	75,000 Dutch
	700 American
Belgium:	62,000 Belgian
	1,300 American
East Germany:	105,000 E. German
	365,000 Soviet
Poland:	220,000 Polish
	45,000 Soviet
Czechoslovakia:	135,000 Czech
	70,000 Soviet
Hungary:	75,000 Hungarian
	60,000 Soviet

Source: *The Military Balance 1977–78* (London: The International Institute for Strategic Studies, 1977) and other sources.

Mutual and Balanced Force Reduction
Issues and Prospects

William B. Prendergast

American Enterprise Institute for Public Policy Research
Washington, D.C.

William B. Prendergast, who has been the U.S. defense adviser to NATO, deputy special assistant to the secretary and the deputy secretary of defense, and associate professor of government at the U.S. Naval Academy, is a government relations consultant.

327.174

P91m

105158

June 1978

ISBN 0-8447-3298-2

AEI Studies 196

Library of Congress Catalog Card No. 78-58589

Printed in the United States of America

THE AEI PUBLIC POLICY PROJECT ON NATIONAL DEFENSE

The American Enterprise Institute,
as part of its foreign policy and
related defense policy study program,
decided in 1976 to establish a defense project
in order to focus public debate on the array of
vital defense issues. The project sponsors research
into strategy, threat, force structure, defense economics,
civil-military relations, and other areas
and presents the results in publications such as
this one and the unique *AEI Defense Review* series.
In addition, it sponsors forums, debates, and conferences,
some of which are televised nationally.

The project is chaired by Melvin R. Laird,
former congressman, secretary of defense,
domestic counsellor to the President, and
now senior counsellor of *Reader's Digest*.
The twenty-four member advisory council
represents a broad range of defense viewpoints.
The project director is Robert J. Pranger,
head of AEI's foreign and defense policy studies program.
General Bruce Palmer, Jr., U.S. Army (retired)
serves as consultant to the chairman.

Views expressed are those of the authors
and do not necessarily reflect the views either
of the advisory council and others associated with
the project or of the advisory panels,
staff, officers, and trustees of AEI.

CONTENTS

PREFACE

On January 31, 1973, representatives of twelve NATO nations and of seven members of the Warsaw Pact assembled in Vienna to open negotiations to prepare for a conference on mutual force reductions in Central Europe. Five years later, as this study was in preparation, the negotiators were still there and still far from any agreement that would reduce the concentration of military power the two alliances maintain between the North Sea and the western border of the Soviet Union.

Even though there has been no agreement, nor even noteworthy progress toward one, there are good reasons for examining the Vienna negotiations. In the first place, the form of the talks makes them unique. It is hard to think of any direct precedent for negotiations between two adversary military alliances for the purpose of agreeing on mutual force reduction. Adding to the unique quality of the talks— and compounding the difficulty of reaching agreement—is the participation of many nations in what is basically a bilateral negotiating process. The talks necessarily have some of the characteristics of multilateral negotiations and involve a decision-making process of extraordinary complexity—at least for the Western nations.

Further, the substance of the negotiations is important. Throughout human history, no region on the face of the earth has been more battle-scarred than Central Europe. At present, no area of comparable size holds as great a concentration of conventional military power as has been assembled in this part of the world. The effort to conclude an agreement to reduce military power here has significance and deserves attention.

In addition to these considerations, the public may be curious about what has been occupying the time of a large group of distinguished diplomats in Vienna for the past five years. This study is designed to aid the nonexpert and nonspecialist in tracing the course of the negotiations and speculating about the question, What next?

1

Background to Vienna

At the Yalta conference in 1945, President Roosevelt told Stalin and Churchill that "the United States would take all reasonable steps to preserve peace, but not at the expense of keeping a large army in Europe, three thousand miles away from home. The American occupation would, therefore, be limited to two years."[1] Churchill was dismayed. Stalin's reaction is not recorded, nor is there a record that he predicted the duration of Soviet occupation of European countries.

Early withdrawal of American forces from Europe continued to be an objective through the first year of the Truman administration. It was believed that the military's role in reshaping Germany into a de-Nazified, demilitarized, democratic, and peace-loving society would soon dwindle and that peace treaties would be concluded with the losers without undue delay. The need for large occupation forces, American or other, was expected to be short-lived.

Little more than a year after V-E Day, this illusion had waned. It became clear that the Russians had settled in for lengthy occupation and were probing for westward expansion of their satellite system. The first public signal of changed expectations on the part of the United States came when Secretary of State James F. Byrnes, speaking in Stuttgart on September 6, 1946, said, "Security forces will probably have to remain in Germany for a long period. . . . We will

---

[1] Winston Churchill, *The Second World War*, vol. 5, *Triumph and Tragedy* (Boston: Houghton Mifflin, 1953), p. 353. Roosevelt told General Marshall that American troops would remain in Europe "for at least one year, maybe two" after the war. Marshall's biographer adds, "No one at the White House, the State Department or the higher levels of the Joint Chiefs of Staff contemplated a strong force glaring at the Russians . . . for twenty-five years." Forrest C. Pogue, *George C. Marshall: Organizer of Victory* (New York: Viking Press, 1973), p. 574.

1

not shirk our duty. We are not withdrawing. We are staying here and will furnish our proportionate share of the security forces."[2]

Western Proposals in the 1940s

Early in 1946, Western powers, led by the United States, sought an agreement with the Soviet Union that would provide a basis for mutual withdrawal of most occupation forces. The American proposal called for a twenty-five-year security treaty between the Soviet Union, France, the United Kingdom, and the United States (later extended to forty years) guaranteeing each other and the rest of Europe against German aggression. Such a treaty, Byrnes reasoned, would eliminate "the need to maintain large armed forces in Germany." In their place, the four powers would keep within Germany only a small force of "technically skilled inspectors" to detect and stop any step toward its remilitarization.[3]

The American proposal was first broached in the fall of 1945 by Secretary Byrnes to Molotov and later to Stalin, and it seemed to attract the Soviet leaders. When it was formally presented, with the support of the British and the French, at the Conference of Foreign Ministers in Paris in April 1946, however, it was met by a number of objections from the Soviet Union. Byrnes's successor, Secretary George C. Marshall, was no more successful when he renewed the security treaty proposal to the Soviet Union at the foreign ministers' conferences in Moscow in the spring of 1947 and again in London in the fall.[4]

The rejection of the security treaty led Byrnes to conclude that "the Soviet High Command or the Politburo . . . did not want the United States involved in the maintenance of European security for the next 25 or 40 years. The pressure of American power would restrict the freedom of action which the Soviet Union, as the predominant military power in Europe, might otherwise enjoy."[5]

Late in 1946, Secretary Byrnes offered an alternative proposal—a simple reduction of occupation forces in Germany and Austria, uncomplicated by other provisions such as a mutual security pact or

---

[2] U.S. State Department, *Germany 1947–1949: The Story in Documents*, State Department Publication 3556 (Washington, D.C., 1950), p. 7.

[3] James F. Byrnes, *Speaking Frankly* (New York: Harper, 1947), p. 172.

[4] U.S. State Department, *Germany 1947–1949*, pp. 57–66; U.S. Congress, Senate, Committee on Foreign Relations, *Documents on Germany 1944–1970*, 92d Cong., 1st sess., May 17, 1971, pp. 81–90.

[5] Byrnes, *Speaking Frankly*, p. 176.

2

peace treaties. "Having . . . realized that a German treaty belonged to the distant future, the United States delegation decided that the next best thing was to try again to reduce occupation forces throughout Europe," Byrnes later wrote.[6] The proposal called on each of the occupying powers to reduce its forces in Austria to 10,000 men and in Germany to 200,000 in the Soviet zone, to 140,000 each in the American and British zones, and to 70,000 in the French zone. The proposed ceilings would have required withdrawing more than 50 percent of the Soviet occupation forces but reducing Western forces by a considerably more modest amount. The American occupation force at the end of 1946 was down to 200,000 and still headed downward.[7]

Both the Byrnes proposal and a renewal of it by Secretary Marshall in March of 1947 in Moscow failed to stimulate Russian interest. Nor were the British or the French particularly interested at the time.[8] From 1948 on, a series of events, highlighted by the coup d'état in Czechoslovakia, the Berlin blockade, and the Korean aggression, created a climate unfavorable to initiatives of this kind, and there were no further offers from the United States, the United Kingdom, and France for mutual troop reduction in Europe until 1954.

The troop reduction proposals made by the United States in the immediate postwar period were based on the proposition that the military forces of the victors remained in Germany to guarantee that Germany would not again threaten its neighbors and the peace of the world. By 1948, however, it was recognized that Western military forces were there less to protect against Germany than to protect West Germany and the rest of Western Europe against the Soviet Union. Although Western troops were in Europe as an instrument of containment, they were too few and too poorly prepared for this role. When NATO was formed in 1949, it had only twelve divisions scattered around Western Europe, and these were undermanned, untrained, uncoordinated, and unequipped for combat. By contrast, Secretary of State Dean Acheson noted the presence of twenty-seven Soviet divisions in East Germany, augmented by 60,000 East German police, who had the look of paramilitary personnel.[9]

In these circumstances, further talk of troop reduction seemed

---

[6] Ibid., p. 166.

[7] Earl F. Ziemke, ed., *The U.S. Army in the Occupation of Germany 1944–1946*, Army Historical Series (Washington, D.C., 1974), p. 423.

[8] Jean Edward Smith, ed., *The Papers of General Lucius D. Clay, Germany 1945–1949*, vol. 1 (Bloomington: Indiana University Press, 1973), pp. 367–68.

[9] Dean Acheson, *Present at the Creation* (New York: Norton, 1968), pp. 436–37.

3

wide of the mark to those in power in Western countries. What was needed was to increase the number and the quality of Western military forces and to establish collective defense arrangements. This was suggested in a speech delivered in the House of Commons by Ernest Bevin on January 22, 1948, which led to the signing of the Brussels Defense Pact two months later. In the following year the North Atlantic Treaty Organization (NATO) came into existence, and serious thought began about rearming the West Germans.

Even after those who governed the major Western powers had lost interest in troop reduction, a new proposal of this type was developed by the State Department's Policy Planning Staff. It was prepared as an option for Secretary Acheson to present at the Conference of Foreign Ministers held in May 1949. This proposal, known as Plan A, called both for a reduction in occupation forces and for their disengagement by withdrawing to the periphery of Germany. British forces were to withdraw to the Hamburg area; American, to the Bremen area; Russian, to the Stettin area; and French, to a point near the Franco-German border.

Plan A was never offered to the Soviet Union. Secretary Acheson wrote that "General Bradley, then Chairman of the Joint Chiefs of Staff . . . pointed out that the result of such an effort would be to back British and American forces into indefensible positions in port areas, while Russian forces would not be moved far enough eastward to make much difference."[10] From Germany, General Clay expressed his opinion of Plan A: "If you really want to turn Germany over to the Soviets, then this is the way to do it."[11]

Eastern Proposals, 1948–1952

As the Western powers turned away from offering troop reduction proposals and began building up their forces, forming a defensive alliance, and relieving West Germany of the restrictions of allied military control, the Eastern European states took up the cause of withdrawing occupation troops and concluding a peace treaty with Germany. The interest of the Soviet Union and its satellites in this cause mounted as West Germany's progress toward political independence, rearmament, and association with the Western military alliance increased.

---

[10] Ibid., pp. 291–92. For a different view, George F. Kennan, *Memoirs* (Boston: Little, Brown, 1967), vol. 1, pp. 427–48.

[11] Smith, *Clay Papers*, vol. 2, p. 1149.

4

In June 1948, the Western occupying powers and the Benelux nations—Belgium, the Netherlands, and Luxembourg—announced their decision to permit the establishment of an autonomous West German government, and the United States Senate adopted the Vandenberg resolution signaling willingness to join a Western military alliance. About two weeks later, the Soviet Union imposed a total land blockade on Berlin. On the same day, June 24, 1948, the foreign ministers of the Eastern European countries, meeting in Warsaw, issued a declaration calling for "a peace treaty with Germany, in accordance with the Potsdam decisions, so that the occupying troops of all the Powers should be withdrawn from Germany within one year after the conclusion of a peace treaty."[12]

In late summer of 1950, after the outbreak of war in Korea, President Truman announced substantial increases in American forces stationed in Western Europe and NATO reached a decision to establish an integrated force under centralized command. This decision came on the eve of action by the French National Assembly endorsing the Pleven plan, which would have included German units in a European army. In response, in Prague on October 21, 1950, the Eastern foreign ministers again called for a German peace treaty and withdrawal of occupation troops.[13]

In February 1952, the Western scheme to create a European Defense Community, which would include German forces, was all but agreed on in London by the foreign ministers of the Big Three. Toward the end of the month, NATO in Lisbon set an ambitious goal for expanding its military forces to ninety-six divisions by 1954. On March 10, the Soviet Union responded by submitting to the West a draft outline of a German peace treaty. The outline provided, as had earlier proposals from the East, for withdrawal of occupation troops and liquidation of foreign military bases in Germany one year after the treaty became effective. This proposal had a new tone, however, and it contained much that would sound attractive to Germans. It jettisoned completely the policies of de-Nazification and demilitarization. It promised Germany reunification (though without describing the process), its own military forces, UN membership, and an end to occupation forces and to economic restrictions. The price to be exacted for these concessions was to be a German "pledge not to enter into any coalitions or military alliances whatsoever directed

---

[12] Royal Institute of International Affairs, *Documents on International Affairs 1947/48* (Oxford: Oxford University Press), pp. 566–74.

[13] Royal Institute of International Affairs, *Documents on International Affairs 1949/50*, p. 167.

5

against any Power which took part with its armed forces in the war against Germany."[14]

The Spirit of Geneva and Force Reduction

New Russian leadership after Stalin's death and the termination of fighting in Korea rekindled hope for resolving some of the problems left over from World War II. In Washington, a new administration undertook the task of working out a more satisfactory *modus vivendi* with the Soviet Union. Its approach was skeptical, but not without hope, and its efforts were prodded along by the British, who were always devising new proposals. Moscow was stimulated to renew its activity toward deterring the developing movement to enlist a re-armed Germany in a Western defense alliance. During the years of the Eisenhower administration, many proposals were offered for troop withdrawals and reductions in Europe. During these years also, a breakthrough came with the conclusion of the Austrian peace treaty, which brought to an end the occupation of this part of Central Europe by the World War II victors.

The basic positions of the Russians and the Western powers un-folded in detail at the Conference of Foreign Ministers in Berlin in early 1954 and at the Geneva summit meeting the following year. Molotov presented two proposals to the Berlin conference. One con-tained the terms of a German peace treaty, and the other, a draft European security treaty.

The essentials of the proposed German peace treaty had not changed since 1952: a reunified Germany within the frontiers estab-lished *de facto* in 1945; a neutralized Germany, forsworn to enter no coalition or alliance against any World War II allied nation; with-drawal from Germany of all occupying forces; and liquidation of foreign military bases in Germany one year after conclusion of the treaty.

The draft European security treaty, however, contained new ele-ments. The gist of the proposal was that the four powers—the Soviet Union, the United States, Great Britain, and France—call a con-

---

[14] Royal Institute of International Affairs, *Documents on International Affairs 1952*, pp. 85–87. The Soviet proposal of 1952 is discussed in Acheson, *Present at the Creation*, pp. 629–32. The West failed to achieve both of the announced goals which prompted the Soviet move in 1952: The European Defense Community was not established, and NATO forces never attained the strength set in the Lisbon force goals.

6

ference of European states to conclude a collective security treaty and begin to withdraw occupation forces. Although some details of the treaty would remain to be worked out at that conference, its thrust was clear. It was to establish a European security system to replace NATO. All European states, "irrespective of their social systems," would be eligible for membership in the new organization, but the United States as a non-European power could participate only in the status of an observer. The Soviet Union obviously would be unchallenged as the dominant military power in such a security system.

The Western nations offered the Eden plan at the Berlin conference. This plan outlined a procedure for the reunification of Germany to be followed by an agreement on limitation of military forces. It conflicted with the Soviet proposals in two important respects: (1) Germany was to be reunified through free elections, and (2) the reunified Germany would enjoy the right to associate itself with other nations in NATO or any other military or political organization.

The 1954 Berlin conference also addressed the subject of an Austrian peace treaty. It appeared that all outstanding issues were resolved, when Molotov made an unexpected announcement that Soviet occupation troops would remain in Austria, even after the conclusion of a peace treaty, until the German issue had been settled. This position was opposed by the Western powers, as well as by Austria, and on this issue the treaty foundered.

Despite the failure to make progress toward peace settlements with Germany and Austria in 1954, the prospects for agreement seemed to brighten in the spring of 1955. Indeed, the Austrian treaty, including the provision for withdrawal of occupation forces, was agreed on in May, and the withdrawal was completed by mid-October. This treaty was concluded with surprising ease and speed once the conference got under way—surprising in view of the tortuous, unsuccessful earlier negotiations on the subject that had involved 379 meetings between the Western powers and the Russians at various levels over a nine-year period. At the time the treaty was concluded, the occupation force in Austria was down to 65,000 troops, about 45,000 of them from the Red Army.

The Soviet Union abandoned its demand that occupation of Austria continue until the conclusion of a German peace treaty. The political price Austria paid for having all occupation forces withdrawn and its independence reestablished was its pledge of permanent neutrality. This pledge was recognized by the United States, the Soviet Union, the United Kingdom, and France and incorporated in a provision of Austria's constitutional law that states that the country "will not join any military alliances and will not permit the establishment of any foreign military bases on her territory."[15]

The settlement of the Austrian problem stimulated hopes that a German treaty and other measures of détente might be agreed upon when the summit meeting of the heads of government of the four powers took place in July at Geneva. The hopes were sustained by the terms of the final communiqué issued at the summit. It directed the foreign ministers of the four powers to consider proposals that had been aired at the conference—a security pact for Europe and various arms limitation schemes, specifically including "the establishment between East and West of a zone in which the disposition of armed forces would be subject to mutual agreement." Most important, the communiqué declared that "the heads of government have agreed the settlement of the German question and the reunification of Germany by free elections shall be carried out in conformity with the national interests of the German people and the interests of European security."

The final communiqué of the summit meeting, however, papered over the profound differences that remained between the Soviet Union and the West. There might have been less optimism and less talk of the "spirit of Geneva" if there had been more understanding that the Russian interpretation of the agreement would reflect the views Bulganin clearly expressed at Geneva. German reunification, "in conformity with . . . the interests of European security," implied to the Russians, at least, a reversal of the step taken two months before the summit—the admission of West Germany to NATO.

Bulganin told his colleagues at Geneva that "the remilitarization of Western Germany and its integration into military groupings of the Western Powers now represent the main obstacles to its unification." He proposed a system of collective security (in which the United States was invited to be a full member) to replace NATO and the newly formed Warsaw Pact. Further, Bulganin declared, "our ultimate objective should be to have no foreign troops remaining on the territories of European states." The Soviet position had not changed, as far as Germany and NATO were concerned, since the

---

[15] Among the works in English treating the Austrian treaty negotiation in detail are Sven Allard, *Russia and the Austrian State Treaty* (University Park, Penn.: Pennsylvania State University Press, 1970); William B. Bader, *Austria Between East and West 1945–55* (Stanford, Calif.: Stanford University Press, 1966); Kurt Waldheim, *The Austrian Example* (New York: Macmillan, 1973).

8

1954 Berlin conference. But Bulganin was now asking for removal of United States forces from all of Europe, not just from Germany.[16]

When the foreign ministers of the four powers convened on October 28, 1955, in Geneva, they had before them the task of giving precision to several general proposals that had been offered at the summit meeting in July. The Western proposal, a refinement of the Eden plan developed first for the 1954 Berlin conference, was presented as an outline of a treaty of assurance on the reunification of Germany. It contained the following noteworthy provision under the heading "Limitation of Forces and Armaments":

> In a zone comprising areas of comparable size and depth and importance on both sides of the line of demarcation between a reunified Germany and the Eastern European countries, levels of armed forces would be specified so as to establish a military balance which would contribute to European security and help to relieve the burden of armaments. There would be appropriate provisions for the maintenance of this balance. In parts of the zone which lie closest to the line of demarcation, there might be special measures relating to the disposition of military forces and installations.

In addition, the Western proposal envisaged control measures to assure that the limitations agreed upon would be observed. These measures were to include exchange of information; mutual inspection, particularly to warn against preparation for surprise attack; and radar warning systems on each side of the line of demarcation to be manned by personnel from the other side.[17]

This proposal is noteworthy because it went beyond suggestions previously offered in negotiations and because it foreshadowed important elements of NATO proposals that would be presented in future negotiations on mutual and balanced force reduction (MBFR). Unlike earlier proposals, the new one was not limited to German territory but aimed at carving out a zone of restricted military power reaching into

---

[16] For accounts of the summit from the Western point of view, see Dwight D. Eisenhower, *Mandate for Change* (New York: Doubleday, 1963), chap. 21; Anthony Eden, *Memoirs: Full Circle* (Boston: Houghton Mifflin, 1960), pp. 319–46; Harold Macmillan, *The Tides of Fortune 1945–1955* (New York: Harper, 1969), pp. 582–628; U.S. State Department, *The Geneva Conference of Heads of Government July 18–23, 1955*, State Department Publication 6046 (Washington, D.C., 1955).

[17] U.S. Congress, Senate, Committee on Foreign Relations, *Documents on Germany 1944–1970*, pp. 233–35, 264–66, 279–84; U.S. State Department, *The Geneva Meeting of Foreign Ministers October 27–November 16, 1955*, State Department Publication 6156 (Washington, D.C., 1955).

9

other countries of Central Europe; it was not limited to withdrawal of foreign forces from the countries affected; and, finally, it defined the objective of force limitation in terms of creating a military balance in Central Europe.

The counterproposal of the Soviet Union was in the form of a draft of a General European Treaty on Collective Security, which "would facilitate the earliest possible settlement of the German problem through the unification of Germany on a peaceful and democratic basis." The treaty was to be open to signature by all European states, including the two Germanies pending unification, and by the United States as well. It provided for the dissolution of both NATO and the Warsaw Pact and created an organization to replace them. It contained a pledge that no nation would increase its forces then stationed on the territory of another state in Europe and envisaged the conclusion of an agreement to withdraw foreign troops from European territory as well as generally to reduce armaments and prohibit atomic weapons.[18]

The idea of withdrawing foreign troops from European soil had been introduced by Bulganin at the Geneva summit meeting. Previous Soviet proposals had dealt with withdrawal of occupation forces from Germany alone. At the summit Bulganin spoke of "withdrawal of foreign troops from the territories of European states and the re-establishment of the situation which existed prior to the Second World War." From 1955 on, Eastern proposals for troop withdrawal used the same formula. Khrushchev, for example, proposed in a 1957 interview granted to American journalists that the United States pull its forces out of West Germany, France, Italy, Turkey, Greece, and "other places where your troops are stationed and of which I do not know." In return, he offered to withdraw Soviet troops from East Germany, Poland, Hungary, and Rumania.[19]

Four years passed before another meeting at Geneva was held, this time in response to a Soviet demand that the occupation of West Berlin be ended. This meeting was a conference of foreign ministers with representatives of the two Germanies in attendance. The offer now made by the three Western powers to the Soviet Union was a modified version of their proposal at the 1955 conference. Like the earlier proposal, it was part of a package, the main element of which was a Germany reunified by free elections and free to participate in

---

[18] U.S. State Department, *The Geneva Meeting*; Senate Foreign Relations Committee, *Documents on Germany*, pp. 236–40, 267–70, 282–83.

[19] Quoted in Eugene Hinterhoff, *Disengagement* (London: Stevens, 1959), pp. 204–5.

10

any military or other organization it wished. This offer went beyond the 1955 proposal, however, by providing that the territory then constituting East Germany would be demilitarized after reunification. It further proposed a zone of controlled armaments between East and West with the line of demarcation to be "mutually determined" and no longer set as the boundary between a reunified Germany and Poland.

The Soviet proposal was an updated version of its earlier proposals for a German treaty, including its provisions requiring the withdrawal of both Germanies from their military alliances and the elimination of foreign forces and bases from Germany. This was no more acceptable to the West than a unified Germany, bound to NATO, was to the East. Unlike the 1954 proposal, however, the draft treaty the Soviet Union presented in 1959 appeared to abandon the goal of German reunification. It envisaged the future of Germany either as a continuation of two individual states or as a confederation of two autonomous political entities.[20]

Again, no progress was made at Geneva.

Proposals from Other Sources

During the 1950s, a spate of ideas for disengagement, troop reduction, safety belts, and atom-free zones came from many sources.[21] The proposal that attracted widest support was the Rapacki plan, which was offered in 1957 by the Polish foreign minister. Rapacki urged the establishment of a denuclearized zone embracing the two Germanies, Poland, and Czechoslovakia. Nuclear weapons would not be manufactured or stockpiled in this zone, installations for their servicing would not be located there, and the use of nuclear weapons against this zone would be prohibited. This plan was intended as a first step toward reducing other kinds of armaments in Central Europe. The Rapacki plan was adopted immediately as part of every disarmament program offered by the Communist world.

Others both in public and in private life also came up with plans. Among them were Belgians Paul Henri Spaak and Paul Van Zeeland; Germans Hermann Rauschning, Eric Mende, Erich Ollenhauer;

---

[20] U.S. State Department, *Foreign Ministers Meeting May–August 1959 Geneva*, State Department Publication 6882 (Washington, D.C., September 1959); G. Bernard Noble, *Christian A. Herter*, vol. 18 of *American Secretaries of State and Their Diplomacy*, Robert H. Ferrell, ed. (New York: Cooper Square Publishers, 1970), chaps. 3–5.

[21] Hinterhoff, *Disengagement*, is a very useful compilation of such proposals.

11

Britons Hugh Gaitskell, Denis Healey, Sir John Slessor, B. H. Liddell Hart; and Americans George Kennan, Henry Reuss, Hubert Humphrey, Henry Kissinger.

The British Labour party and the British Trade Union Congress in 1958 gave formal approval to a plan of disengagement in Central Europe prepared by Hugh Gaitskell and Denis Healey. This plan combined neutralization of the two Germanies, as well as Poland, Czechoslovakia, and Hungary, with demilitarization under international guarantee.

In 1959, the Social Democratic party of Germany unveiled the Deutschland plan. It proposed, as a first step, establishing a zone of relaxation which would include both Germanies, Poland, Czechoslovakia, and Hungary. All foreign troops would be withdrawn from this zone, and it would be denuclearized. At the same time, a collective security convention would be signed by all European states. In a second step, Germany would be reunited.

Henry Kissinger in an article entitled "The Search for Stability," published in *Foreign Affairs* in July 1959, proposed that non-German forces in both Germanies be pulled back. In the west, such forces were to be withdrawn to the Weser River; in the east, to the Vistula in Poland. Further, the manpower and equipment of German, Czech, and Polish forces were to be brought into balance.

NATO's Developing Interest in Mutual Force Reduction

In the first years of the 1960s, the West showed no inclination to talk about troop reduction in Europe. Soviet threats to Berlin, culminating in the construction of the wall in 1961, and the Cuban missile crisis the following year raised new fears of a more aggressive Soviet foreign policy. Also, NATO, prodded by the United States, slowly began to realize that nuclear capability could not much longer be its chief instrument to deter aggression and to accept the need for greater conventional strength to provide deterrence without the threat of using nuclear weapons at the outset of conflict. These factors all impelled the West to think for a time of augmenting, instead of reducing, its forces.

At Oslo in May 1961, Secretary Rusk urged upon his fellow foreign ministers an increase in NATO divisions from the twenty-one then in existence to twenty-seven or thirty and pledged the commitment of five Polaris submarines to the alliance. One year later, in response to heightened tension over Berlin, the United States added

50,000 men to its forces in Europe, bringing the total to almost 420,000, with 280,000 in Germany. Although the response of other nations was less dramatic, nevertheless in March of 1962 General Lauris Norstad, the supreme Allied commander in Europe, announced that Western military strength in Central Europe had grown by 25 percent in one year's time. In view of this increase, Norstad said, "We now definitely can think in terms of a true forward strategy."[22]

During the early 1960s, the Soviet Union continued to issue intermittent calls for withdrawal of foreign troops from Europe. In a letter to President Kennedy dated February 21, 1962, for example, Khrushchev deplored "the refusal of the Western Powers to relax even in the smallest degree the intensity of their military preparations; for example, to abolish military bases on the territories of foreign States and to withdraw their troops from Europe to their own territory." Khrushchev added, "The Soviet Union is prepared to repatriate immediately its troops now stationed abroad, if the Western Powers will do the same."[23]

The year 1963 brought some signs of a thaw in the relations between the United States and the Soviet Union and a reversal of the American military buildup in Europe. From the high point in 1962, the United States forces in Europe were cut over the course of four years by 100,000 or approximately 25 percent. There is evidence that President Kennedy sought to bring about force reduction on both sides by informing the Soviet Union in 1963 that the United States would reduce its forces in Europe and inviting the Russians to do the same. It has been suggested that a withdrawal of 14,000 Soviet troops from East Germany occurred in 1964 and that it was a response to an American reduction of 8,000 soldiers in April of that year;[24] the evidence is less than conclusive, however. If, in fact, the "policy of mutual example," as it has been called, was followed in this instance by the major powers, its success was limited. The Soviet Union did not respond in kind to other, larger reductions made in American forces in Western Europe during the 1960s.

How serious either the United States or the Soviet Union was in late 1963 in probing the subject of force reductions is far from clear. Whatever the attitude of the superpowers at that time, the European NATO nations clearly were not then interested in the subject. Later

---

[22] "Norstad says forces have been reinforced 25 percent but more must be done," *New York Times*, March 24, 1962.

[23] U.S. Arms Control and Disarmament Agency, *Documents on Disarmament 1962*, vol. 1 (Washington, D.C., 1963), p. 55.

[24] David Linebaugh, "We Cut, You Cut," *New York Times*, October 5, 1976.

13

in the decade, though, there was a sharp change of attitude on the part of the alliance. In the spring of 1967, the NATO council, meeting in Luxembourg, for the first time included in its communiqué a cautious expression of interest in achieving mutual force reductions.[25] The communiqué stated:

> If conditions permit, a balanced reduction of forces by the East and West could be a significant step toward security in Europe. A contribution on the part of the Soviet Union and the Eastern European countries towards a reduction of forces would be welcomed as a gesture of peaceful intent.

This language was echoed in the NATO communiqué of December 1967 after a meeting in Brussels. It was at this meeting that the NATO foreign ministers adopted the report on *The Future Tasks of the Alliance*, known as the Harmel report after the Belgian foreign minister who had proposed the project. In elevating the pursuit of détente to the same level as the attainment of military strength, the Harmel report signaled a reorientation of NATO objectives. It asserted that the purpose of collective defense is to serve as a stabilizing factor to make possible effective policies directed toward a greater relaxation of tensions. "The way to peace and stability in Europe rests in particular on the use of the Alliance constructively in the interest of détente," the report declared. "Military security and a policy of détente are not contradictory but complementary."[26] The ministers reported that the Allies were engaging in study of disarmament and practical arms control measures, "including the possibility of balanced force reductions."

Six months later at Reykjavik, the representatives of NATO countries participating in its defense program issued a declaration entitled *Mutual and Balanced Force Reductions*. The declaration laid down certain "agreed principles" which would govern alliance studies of the subject, and it issued an invitation to the East in these words:

> Ministers agreed that it was desirable that a process leading to mutual force reductions should be initiated. To that end they decided to make all necessary preparations for discussions on this subject with the Soviet Union and other countries of Eastern Europe and they call on them to join in this search for progress towards peace.

---

[25] This and subsequent quotations from NATO ministerial communiqués are published in *NATO Final Communiqués 1949–1974* (Brussels: NATO Information Service, 1975).

[26] *NATO Handbook* (Brussels: NATO Information Service, 1976).

14

At every subsequent NATO ministerial meeting, with one exception, the invitation to the Soviet Union and its allies was pressed. The exception came in 1968 following the Soviet invasion of Czechoslovakia. This action, the NATO ministers asserted, was a severe setback to prospects for mutual balanced force reductions. Nevertheless, studies and preparations were to go on, awaiting a more favorable atmosphere for fruitful negotiation.

The effort begun by the NATO nations in 1967 to engage the Warsaw Pact in discussions of mutual force reduction was a response to a combination of pressures. The mood of détente was on the rise. For ten years the Soviet Union had refrained from disturbing the peace of Europe by military action. The blood in the streets of Budapest had been forgotten. The United States talked of building bridges with the East. Agreements were multiplying between East and West. Increasing contacts were made through cracks in the iron curtain. A new German government in Bonn was busy promoting human, economic, and cultural contacts with the German Democratic Republic—a policy endorsed by the NATO ministers in December 1966. Fissures were appearing in the Communist world, ranging from Chinese hostility toward Moscow to a subtle drift toward autonomy on the part of Czechoslovakia and Rumania. In short, the East no longer looked so threatening.

In the West, strength and cohesion seemed to be slipping. Economic and political strains weakened enthusiasm among the people of the NATO nations for maintaining alliance troop strength and defense budget levels. The United States, beginning in 1965, plunged with massive military force into Vietnam. This war not only distracted U.S. attention from Europe but also drew some of its forces from there, and in time nurtured a feeling among Americans that they were overcommitted militarily throughout the world. Quarrels spread within NATO. America's allies were dissatisfied with its Vietnam policy, and the Johnson administration complained that the European allies were doing too little in the common defense. The United States became alarmed about inflation and its balance of payments with the rest of the world. Its European allies replied that they had economic problems, too, and balked at helping to solve America's. Finally, in 1966 and 1967, NATO's defenses seemed to be at the point of beginning to unravel.

The most serious setback was the withdrawal of France from the military activities of the alliance in May 1966. The potential impact of this French dissociation can be gauged from the fact that more than one-third of the military manpower in NATO's central area was

15

French. Though France had no intention of disarming or withdrawing its forces from Germany, its considerable military strength no longer could be counted on as part of the forces available for any coordinated defense of Western Europe. Further, the forced removal of NATO headquarters and other installations from France raised a big question about the future availability of French territory to the United States and other NATO nations in time of crisis or conflict.

At the same time, other NATO countries were contemplating, or preparing for, reductions in their forces. On February 16, 1967, the United Kingdom published a Defense White Paper pointing toward accelerated application of a 1966 decision to cut forces in the Far East and the Middle East and casting doubt on the future of 51,000 British troops in West Germany. The White Paper not only argued for an extension of détente through mutual reductions by both NATO and the Warsaw Pact, but also implied that without adequate German financial assistance, unilateral reductions would be necessary to offset the cost of maintaining the British Army of the Rhine.[27]

The United States had already cut its troop strength in Europe by 100,000 since 1962, and pressed by escalating demands in Vietnam and balance of payments problems, it was talking of further force reductions. It, too, sought more financial help from Bonn. From late 1966 until mid-1967, American and British representatives negotiated with the West German government, finally producing an agreement which alleviated the adverse balance of payments impact of stationing troops in Germany.

Nevertheless, both British and American troops on the spot in Germany were reduced further after January 1, 1968. With NATO concurrence, a policy of dual basing was adopted for somewhat more than 10 percent of the land and air forces Great Britain and the United States then had stationed in continental Europe. The dual-based forces were to be withdrawn from Germany to their homelands. They were to remain fully committed to NATO, however, were to return to Germany yearly for exercises, and were to be kept at a high degree of readiness for speedy movement to Europe in an emergency.

West Germany, the other major prop in the alliance, was also contemplating cuts in its military forces—a reduction in manpower from 461,000 to 400,000 over the course of several years. The reduction did not get beyond the planning stage. The displeasure in Washington produced by reports of German cuts led to a meeting

---

[27] Ministry of Defence, *Statement on the Defence Estimates 1967* (London: Her Majesty's Stationery Office, 1967), p. 6.

16

between Chancellor Kiesinger and President Johnson at which they affirmed that there should be consultation and agreement in the alliance before either country again proposed to reduce forces committed to NATO.[28]

Activities in the United States Senate also affected the atmosphere in which NATO embarked on its campaign to engage the Warsaw Pact in discussions on force reduction. In August 1966, Senator Mansfield, leader of the majority in the Senate, offered a resolution calling for a "substantial reduction of U.S. forces permanently stationed in Europe." Resubmitted in 1967 with the support of forty-three senators, it was the subject of protracted hearings by a special Senate committee in the spring of that year. Although the Johnson administration opposed the Mansfield resolution, it did respond to congressional pressure by adopting the dual-basing scheme, which had the effect of reducing the American troop presence in Europe by 35,000, and by concluding the 1967 offset agreement with the Federal Republic of Germany. In subsequent years, Mansfield's persistence in pressing for further troop reduction was a constant threat that additional cuts might occur.

Thus, there were multiple signs that progressive enfeeblement of the NATO military posture was taking place. When NATO proposed mutual troop reduction to the Warsaw Pact, its negotiating position was anything but strong, and it is not surprising that the Pact ignored NATO's invitation. The East may well have felt in the late 1960s that there was no reason to pay for a NATO reduction which in all likelihood would take place unilaterally.

Three years of being ignored by the Warsaw Pact did not dull NATO's persistence. In 1969 from Brussels, the Reykjavik invitation to discuss mutual force reduction was renewed. In May of 1970 at Rome, the NATO ministers issued a new declaration on MBFR, which laid down four governing principles of NATO's negotiating position. The declaration also invited "interested states" to hold exploratory talks on force reductions in Europe "with special reference to the Central Region." At long last, in June 1970 an indirect response came from a meeting of the Warsaw Pact foreign ministers in Budapest. The ministers proposed discussing "reduction of foreign armed forces" in Europe but indicated a preference for delaying such a discussion until after the conclusion of a conference on European security.[29]

---

28 *New York Times*, July 7, August 16, and August 22, 1967.
29 Robin A. Remington, *The Warsaw Pact: Case Studies in Communist Conflict Resolution* (Cambridge, Mass.: MIT Press, 1971), pp. 240–42.

17

The conference on European security, which had been advocated by the East for several years, was intended to confirm the map of Europe and the political arrangements in Eastern Europe that had developed after the war.[30] Its purpose was to ratify and declare permanent the Oder-Niesse border between Poland and Germany, the division of Germany into two states, and the political and social systems of East Germany and other Eastern European countries. It was also intended to weaken the NATO alliance and the ties of Western Europe with the United States. In comparison with these objectives, force reduction negotiations with NATO were of minor interest to the Soviet Union. The West—particularly West Germany—in addition to its interest in MBFR, attached great importance to making arrangements which would stabilize the situation in West Berlin and avoid the crises which periodically placed the city in a state of siege.

In a series of cautious and interrelated steps in 1970 and 1971, NATO and the Warsaw Pact moved toward negotiation on force reduction in Central Europe. In August 1970, the Brandt government concluded treaties with the Soviet Union and Poland, accepting the postwar boundaries and the political status quo, thus satisfying a major demand of the Soviet Union. In May 1971, Brezhnev, speaking in Tiflis, invited the West to "taste the wine" of talks on reduction of armed forces and armaments in Central Europe. NATO designated its former secretary general, Manlio Brosio, as its "explorer," commissioned to contact the Soviet Union and other interested governments in order to bring about such negotiations. In late 1971, a complex of agreements on Berlin was concluded—a quadripartite agreement involving the four major powers and understandings between the two Germanies. This satisfied a Western demand for assurances that West Berlin no longer be subject to recurring Soviet and East German pressure to isolate it from West Germany and the rest of the Western world.[31]

Bilateral negotiations between the United States and the Soviet

---

[30] Robert Legvold, "European Security Conference," *Survey* (Summer 1970), pp. 41–52; A. Ross Johnson, "The Warsaw Pact's Campaign for European Security," RAND Paper R-565-PR (Santa Monica: RAND, 1970); Timothy W. Stanley, *A European Security Conference? Problems, Prospects, and Pitfalls* (Washington, D.C.: Atlantic Council, 1970).

[31] U.S. State Department, *United States Foreign Policy 1971: A Report of the Secretary of State*, State Department Publication 8634 (Washington, D.C., 1972), pp. 39–47; Werner Burmeister, "Brandt's Opening to the East," *The Year Book of World Affairs 1973* (London: Stevens and Sons, 1973), pp. 24–38; Lawrence L. Whetten, *Germany's Ostpolitik: Relations Between the Federal Republic and the Warsaw Pact Countries* (Oxford: Oxford University Press, 1971); Dennis L. Bark, *Agreement on Berlin* (Washington, D.C.: American Enterprise Institute, 1974).

Union played a decisive part in bringing about the multilateral talks on force reduction. At the May 1972 Moscow summit meeting at which the Strategic Arms Limitation Treaty was signed, it was agreed that a conference on security and cooperation in Europe should be convened "without undue delay" and that agreements on the procedures for negotiating a troop reduction in Central Europe in a special forum "should be reached as soon as practicable." The bargain thus struck drew each side into a negotiation for which it had little enthusiasm in exchange for a negotiation it desired.[32]

One week after the Moscow summit, the North Atlantic Council meeting in Brussels noted in its communiqué the progress in East-West relations—the SALT agreement, the treaties of the Federal Republic of Germany with the East, and the quadripartite and other agreements on Berlin. "In the light of these favourable developments," the communiqué continued, "ministers agreed to enter into multilateral conversations concerned with preparations for a Conference on Security and Co-operation in Europe."

The NATO ministers evidenced a certain wariness about the understanding on force reduction negotiations that Nixon and Brezhnev had reached at Moscow. Brezhnev had not responded to the NATO invitation nor had he deigned to treat with NATO's emissary, Manlio Brosio. Possibly what Brezhnev had in mind was a bilateral reduction arrangement with the United States, freezing Western Europe out. Or Brezhnev, being assured of his Conference on Security and Cooperation in Europe, might stall indefinitely on a meeting to discuss force reduction. These concerns can be read between the lines of the NATO ministers' pronouncement that they:

> continue to aim at negotiations on mutual and balanced force reductions and related measures. They believe that these negotiations should be conducted on a multilateral basis and be preceded by suitable explorations. They regretted that the Soviet Government has failed to respond to the Allied offer of October 1971 to enter exploratory talks. They therefore now propose that multilateral explorations on mutual and balanced force reductions be undertaken as soon as practicable, either before or in parallel with multilateral preparatory talks on a Conference on Security and Co-operation in Europe.

It took one more trip to the Soviet Union—this time by Secretary Kissinger in mid-September 1972—to pin down the timing of the

---

[32] *U.S. Foreign Policy for the 1970s: Shaping a Durable Peace*, a Report to the Congress by Richard Nixon, May 3, 1973, pp. 14–18, 33–34.

19

talks on force reduction and assure a beginning for MBFR before the security conference settled any major problems. When the North Atlantic Council next met, in December of 1972, the Conference on Security and Cooperation in Europe had opened in Helsinki with thirty-five nations in attendance. The MBFR preparatory talks were scheduled to open in Geneva on January 31, 1973, a date which had been fixed in conversations between the United States and the Soviet Union. On November 15, 1972, the seven NATO nations with troops in the area under discussion had invited Czechoslovakia, the German Democratic Republic, Hungary, Poland, and the Soviet Union to participate in the talks. No response came from the invitees for more than two months. When it arrived—only twelve days before the scheduled opening of the talks—it accepted the date but nothing else. The Warsaw Pact said the meeting place should be Vienna, not Geneva, and the list of participants should be enlarged to include "all interested European states." Further, the talks should be strictly limited to the preparations for later substantive negotiations.

Uncertainty remained until the very eve of the first session. NATO accepted Vienna as the conference site and cancelled its arrangements in Geneva. It rejected, however, the proposal to invite all of Europe. When the NATO representatives left for Vienna, they were still unsure whom they would meet there or whether the talks would surmount the problem of who the participants would be. It was not until January 30, 1973, that the *New York Times* could announce in headlines "Negotiators Clear Away Last Obstacles."[33] With Rumania and Bulgaria added to the list of participants from the East and five additional countries from NATO's northern and southern flanks, the MBFR preparatory negotiations got off on schedule to an uncertain start.

Some Conclusions

By the time the Vienna negotiations opened in early 1973, there had been more than a quarter of a century of discussion from both East and West on the matter of mutual force reductions in Europe. Only in the case of Austria was any agreement achieved.

There is still no universally accepted explanation of why the Soviet Union agreed to withdraw its occupation force from Austria as part of the peace settlement of 1955. Initially the Soviets probably sought to use a relatively mild Austrian peace treaty as a means of derailing the movement of West Germany into NATO, but the con-

---

[33] *New York Times*, January 30, 1973.

20

clusion of the treaty did not come until after Bonn had taken this step. Possibly, it was felt in Moscow that the Austrian example might still in time wean the West Germans, then seriously divided about the wisdom of joining the alliance, away from their ties with the West. At any rate, a neutral Austria was no more disadvantageous to the Soviet Union than an Austria in which Russian occupation forces were rubbing elbows with American troops.[34]

It is clear why mutual force reduction proposals for the rest of Central Europe did not lead to agreement. Most proposals from both sides were offered as part of a package designed to settle "the German problem." The sharp differences between the Soviet Union and the Western powers about the political system and the relationships of postwar Germany were an insurmountable obstacle to agreement. In fact, when negotiations were undertaken, they never even reached the question of troop reductions. In the various major proposals discussed by diplomats, troop reductions were usually step number two in a process that began with German reunification or a German peace treaty. An impasse on step number one always ended negotiations.

Chancellor Brandt's *Ostpolitik* of 1970 narrowed the differences between the two sides. The existence of two Germanies was accepted, and existing borders in Eastern Europe were confirmed by international agreement. These victories for the East were balanced to a degree by agreement on the problems of access to Berlin and by the Soviet Union's apparent abandonment of demands for complete withdrawal of American forces from Europe and for the dissolution of NATO.

Neither side went to Vienna with the kind of enthusiasm that springs from deep conviction about the intrinsic merit of the undertaking; both were under some form of compulsion. The Soviet Union came with reluctance and disinterest, a participant only because this was in exchange for the Conference on Security and Cooperation in Europe, which it strongly desired. If there were to be discussions of mutual troop reduction, Brezhnev would have preferred to conduct

---

[34] Allard, *Russia and the Austrian State Treaty*, pp. 231–38, distinguishes two phases of Russian policy. In the first, the prospect of evacuation of Austria was "a pawn in the game of preventing German rearmament." When this game was lost, the Austrian peace treaty served the Soviets by promoting the idea of neutrality, undermining NATO, and keeping the Third World out of the Western camp.

An editorial in *Pravda*, April 11, 1956, suggested there was some hope that the Austrian example might still reverse the course of West German policy; it asserted that "people in Western Germany are beginning to ponder this example . . . why must the German Federal Republic reject such a policy? Why must it contribute vast sums to the arms race and restrict its sovereignty for the benefit of the military bloc of the Western powers?" (Quoted in Bader, *Austria Between East and West*, p. 206).

21

them with the United States rather than with NATO. The NATO nations, for their part, were under pressure to find cheaper means of maintaining their security. The United Kingdom, which was suffering from chronic economic strain in the postwar years, had a twenty-year history of active and persistent effort in the cause of mutual troop reduction. Anthony Eden devised the Western proposals of 1954 and 1955; Harold Macmillan, those of 1959; and Britain's Defense White Paper of February 1967 was not unrelated to NATO's original call for MBFR negotiations. The administration in Washington, as it moved toward negotiations, felt the hot breath of Senator Mansfield calling for troop withdrawal. Several other NATO nations also were being pressed, in varying degrees, by parliaments and public to make cutbacks in defense establishments.

If either side went to the bargaining table in Vienna at a disadvantage, it was the West. The dominant view in Brussels had consistently been that NATO was inferior to the East in conventional military strength, and there was reason to believe that NATO was on the road to unilateral force reductions. Furthermore, the NATO nations—democracies all—had to negotiate under all the disadvantages that come with frequent elections and accountability of public officials to citizens. When public opinion is impatient for results, as it often is, whether for détente or for relief from tax burdens or for less involvement abroad, negotiators who represent a democracy find their endurance restricted, and it is hard for them to say no indefinitely to risks they initially may reject.

For these and other reasons, the West was pessimistic about the chances of an acceptable agreement. One year to the day before the opening meeting in Vienna, the *New York Times* reported, "After months of study, Nixon administration officials have concluded that any agreement on mutual reduction of forces in Europe that would be likely to be accepted by the Soviet bloc would probably jeopardize Western security." An unnamed State Department official was quoted as saying, "The thing has been wargamed to death, and any conceivable formula always works out against NATO."[35]

A tremendous gap separated the two sides on the issues to be addressed in the Vienna negotiations. There was no prior meeting of the minds, no spadework in advance to establish a basis for agreement. The conference had to start from scratch. Thus, when the representatives of the two alliances assembled in Vienna for their first session, it was clear that they would be there for a long time.

---

[35] *New York Times*, January 31, 1972.

22

2
The Substance of the Negotiations

The exploratory talks between NATO and the Warsaw Pact on mutual force reductions, which opened on January 31, 1973, ended five months later with a decision to enter upon the negotiations proper in Vienna on October 30.[1] In the exploratory talks, both sides agreed on the following principles:

- The general objective of the negotiations is to contribute to a more stable relationship and to the strengthening of peace and security in Europe without diminishing the security of any party to the negotiations.

- The subject matter of the negotiations is to be "mutual reduction of forces and armaments and associated measures in Central Europe."

---

[1] The literature on the MBFR negotiations is not plentiful. Worth reading are John N. Yochelson, "MBFR: The Search for an American Approach," *Orbis*, vol. 17, no. 1 (Spring 1973), pp. 155–75; Yochelson, "MFR: West European and American Perspectives," in *The United States and Western Europe*, Wolfram Hanrieder, ed. (Cambridge, Mass.: Winthrop, 1974), pp. 251–81; Christop Bertram, "Mutual Force Reduction in Europe: The Political Aspects," *Adelphi Paper 84* (London: International Institute for Strategic Studies, 1972); John Erickson, "MBFR: Force Levels and Security Requirements," *Strategic Review* (Summer 1973), pp. 28–43; Thomas W. Wolfe, "Soviet Attitudes toward MBFR and the USSR's Military Presence in Europe," RAND Paper P-4819 (Santa Monica: RAND Corporation, 1972); Lothar Ruehl, "The Negotiations on Force Reductions in Central Europe," *NATO Review*, vol. 24, no. 5, October 1976, pp. 18–25; P. Terrence Hopmann, *Bargaining Within and Between Alliances on MBFR* (Minneapolis: University of Minnesota, 1977). Two useful articles in German are Lothar Ruehl, "Die Wiener Verhandlungen über einen Truppenabbau in Mitteleuropa," *Europa-Archiv*, vol. 13 (1977), pp. 399–408; and Uwe Nerlich, "Die Politik des Streitkrafteabbaus in Europa," *Europa-Archiv*, vol. 7 (1977), pp. 197 ff.

- The area of force reduction is the territory of seven countries: the two Germanies; the Western states of Belgium, the Netherlands, and Luxembourg; and the Eastern states of Poland and Czechoslovakia.

It was also agreed that two categories of participants would be established, direct and special. The direct participants would be the nations having troops in the area of reduction: the United States, the United Kingdom, Canada, the Federal Republic of Germany, and the Benelux countries on the Western side; the Soviet Union, the German Democratic Republic, Poland, and Czechoslovakia on the Eastern side. On the NATO side, the special participants would be Norway, Denmark, Italy, Greece, and Turkey; the special participants representing the Warsaw Pact would be Hungary, Romania, and Bulgaria.

Disagreement on two points surfaced in the exploratory talks. One concerned the use of the word "balanced" in describing the subject matter of the negotiations. The East refused to accept the word. In NATO circles, the topic of the negotiations had always been MBFR—Mutual and Balanced Force Reductions. What was at stake was not a matter of semantics. The disagreement concerned the basic premise on which reduction proposals were to be based—whether an imbalance existed between the forces of the two sides which should be rectified by mutual reductions. The West yielded on this matter and accepted a title for the negotiations which did not mention balance.

There was disagreement, too, about whether the territory of Hungary should be included in the area for reductions—a position favored by NATO and opposed by the Warsaw Pact. On this issue, compromise of a sort was achieved. Negotiations were to proceed with the territory of Hungary excluded, but the Western powers reserved the right to raise the question later in the negotiations.

NATO's Negotiating Position

The issues to be dealt with in the negotiations had received consideration in the West for several years. Official studies of MBFR had been launched in Brussels in 1968 and continued without interruption. Further, a great variety of possible proposals had been examined in the national capitals of the major NATO powers.

In two declarations of the NATO foreign ministers—in Reykjavik in 1968 and in Rome in 1970—guiding principles were laid down to

24

indicate the kind of force reduction agreement the West should seek. As expressed in Rome, these principles were:

(a) Mutual force reductions should be compatible with the vital security interests of the Alliance and should not operate to the military disadvantage of either side having regard for the differences arising from geographical and other considerations.

(b) Reductions should be on a basis of reciprocity, and phased and balanced as to their scope and timing.

(c) Reductions should include stationed and indigenous forces and their weapons systems in the area concerned.

(d) There must be adequate verification and controls to ensure the observance of agreements on mutual and balanced force reductions.

Previously, at Reykjavik, the ministers had affirmed "that the overall military capability of NATO should not be reduced except as part of a pattern of mutual force reductions balanced in scope and timing." This commitment, although not uniformly respected, has nevertheless been a significant deterrent to unilateral force reduction on the part of members of the alliance. This pledge has been renewed repeatedly at subsequent NATO ministerial meetings.[2] The attempt to ensure a common approach was reinforced by an understanding that those from Western nations engaged in the Vienna negotiations, though representing their individual countries, would be subject to NATO control exercised by the Permanent Representatives of the members of the alliance in Brussels.

The Warsaw Pact Proposals

Warsaw Pact deliberations are not as open as those of NATO, and very little is known in the West about preconference preparations and understandings among Pact members.[3] That preparation had taken place was clear from the fact that on November 8, 1973, shortly after the opening of the Vienna conference, a draft agreement of ten articles was introduced by the Warsaw Pact nations.

---

[2] The Reykjavik and Rome communiqués of the NATO foreign ministers are published in *Texts of Final Communiqués 1949–1974* (Brussels: NATO Information Service), pp. 206–10 and 233–38, respectively.

[3] The essentials of the proposals of the Warsaw Pact and NATO covered here and in the following pages have been widely published. One source is the annual *Military Balance* of the International Institute for Strategic Studies (London).

The East's draft agreement proposed equal percentage reductions on both sides of roughly 16 percent of troop strength in the reduction area, including air as well as ground forces and nuclear weapons as well as conventional arms. Specifically, the proposal called for reduction in three stages, beginning in 1975 with a cut of 20,000 men from each side. Later explanation indicated that what was contemplated was a reduction of 10,000 Russians, 5,000 East Germans, and 5,000 other Eastern Europeans from Warsaw Pact forces and 10,000 Americans, 5,000 West Germans, and 5,000 other Western troops from NATO forces. In the second stage in 1976, each side would further cut its troop strength in the area by 5 percent, and in the third stage in 1977, by 10 percent. The second- and third-stage cuts were to apply to all direct participants in the negotiations. Entire units were to be reduced as well as all their equipment.

A supplementary protocol, which would constitute an integral part of the agreement, was to list the units to be reduced along with their equipment. In the case of forces from nations outside the reduction area, withdrawal was required; in the case of the forces of nations within the reduction area, however, the units were to be disbanded and their equipment decommissioned.

The forces on both sides within the reduction area were to be frozen at the levels achieved by the reduction. Each nation would be subject to individual manpower and equipment ceilings within the reduction area.

NATO's First Proposal

On November 22, the NATO nations offered a proposal that was less comprehensive than that which the Warsaw Pact had put forth. It called for reduction of ground forces in Central Europe to a ceiling set illustratively at 700,000 men on each side. The cut to this level was to be achieved in two phases: first, a withdrawal of a designated number of American and Soviet ground forces and later a reduction of the troops of other nations.

In Phase I, 68,000 Soviet ground troops, including a Soviet tank army with 1,700 tanks and all its other equipment, were to be withdrawn. This constituted about 15 percent of Soviet ground force personnel in the reduction area, according to NATO estimates. The United States would at the same time withdraw an equal percentage of its ground troops—29,000 men—but with no specification as to type and no requirement that any complete unit or any equipment be withdrawn. In Phase II the further reductions required to bring the forces of each side down to the common ceiling would be made.

The differences between the initial proposals of the two sides at Vienna were substantial. The outcome of the Pact proposal would be to maintain the existing manpower ratio between the two military forces. According to NATO figures, at the opening of the negotiations Warsaw Pact forces in Central Europe outnumbered those of the alliance by 150,000. If these figures are accepted, the result of adopting the Pact's reduction plan would be numerical superiority for the East of approximately 125,000. This imbalance would be perpetuated for a period of many years by international agreement.

The Western proposal aimed at an outcome that would establish equality in numbers of ground forces on both sides after Phase II. This, according to NATO's figures, would require unequal reductions—77,000 Western troops and 225,000 Pact troops. NATO ground forces were to be reduced by 10 percent of the total number based in Central Europe at the outset of the negotiations whereas Warsaw Pact ground forces were to be trimmed by 24 percent. Although NATO's proposal left room for modifying the ceiling figure of 700,000 men, the West decided that its reductions would not exceed 10 percent of its ground forces in Central Europe and that the Pact would be expected to make whatever reduction was required to bring its forces down to the level of parity.

The second most significant difference between the two proposals lay in the nature of the ceiling each envisaged. NATO's plan called for a collective ceiling; it did not impose a limit on the size of the forces of any individual nation so long as the ground forces on its side, taken together, did not exceed the total of 700,000. The Warsaw Pact plan, on the other hand, imposed eleven individual national ceilings.

A third point of difference is that under the Western plan, as compared with that of the Warsaw Pact, a significantly larger share of the reductions made in NATO force levels would be in U.S. forces. Thirty-eight percent of the total Western reduction would be taken in the first phase of the NATO proposal, in which only American troops would be cut from the Western forces. Because American forces constitute only 25 percent of NATO's total ground force strength in Central Europe, the ultimate result would be smaller percentage reductions for the European allies than for the United States.

The Warsaw Pact proposal would lead to approximately the same numerical reduction in American forces as the NATO proposal, but it would take 75 percent of the total NATO reduction from European forces as opposed to about 60 percent under NATO's plan. In

27

this respect, the Eastern proposal seems inconsistent with the previous position of the Soviet Union, which repeatedly during the 1950s and 1960s called for complete withdrawal of American forces from Europe. In the MBFR talks, however, the East is emphasizing a different objective—reducing the largest NATO forces, those of West Germany, and setting a ceiling on their size for the future.

It is not possible to compare how the structure of Warsaw Pact forces would be affected by Eastern and Western proposals, because it is not clear how the second phase of NATO's plan would apportion reductions among Warsaw Pact forces. Under the Warsaw Pact reduction plan, however, Soviet ground troops would continue to constitute 50 percent of the Eastern force.

An additional point of difference in the two proposals was that the Eastern plan applied not only to ground forces and conventional weapons but also to air forces and to nuclear arms. It also required reduction of complete units and of all arms and equipment associated with forces that are removed or disbanded. Although the Western proposal required the removal of the troops and equipment of one Soviet tank army, it said nothing about removing complete Western units or the equipment associated with troops cut from NATO forces.

Neither side could have expected that its original offer would be acceptable to the other without substantial modification. In fact, a fallback position had been developed within the United States government even before the preparatory talks in Vienna began. It might reasonably have been expected that the Warsaw Pact similarly would have in reserve proposals more palatable to the West, which would be presented in the course of the negotiations. In December 1975, the NATO nations did offer new proposals which significantly changed their original plan. The Pact nations made their second proposal two months later.

NATO's Offer of 1975

On December 16, 1975, the NATO side added a concession to its original offer in the form of its so-called Option III.[4] In addition to the withdrawal of 29,000 American soldiers, the United States declared its willingness to withdraw from the reduction area 1,000 of

---

[4] The United States introduced three possible reduction proposals for consideration by NATO in 1973 at the time of decision on the nature of the proposal to be made in the Vienna negotiations. The proposal made in 1975 was the third on this list of options.

its nuclear warheads together with certain delivery systems: 54 nuclear-capable F-4 aircraft and 36 Pershing missile launchers. At the same time, the NATO nations expressed willingness to accept a manpower ceiling of 900,000 on each side, which would include both ground and air personnel. Since NATO's estimates were that each side had 200,000 air force personnel in the reduction area, this proposal did not require any greater total manpower reduction than did the original Western proposal but opened up the possibility of some cuts in air forces as well as ground troops.

The Warsaw Pact Offer of 1976

The Warsaw Pact responded on February 19, 1976, with an addition to the draft agreement it put forth when the negotiations began. In an apparent concession to the Western position, the proposal provided for reduction in two phases, with only the forces of the United States and the Soviet Union affected in the first phase. This phase, which the Warsaw Pact wished to implement in 1976, would involve a reduction of American and Soviet troops equal in amount to 2 to 3 percent of each side's total troop strength. In addition, one army corps headquarters, 300 tanks on each side, 54 nuclear-capable F-4s and SU 17/20 A and C aircraft, and 36 Pershing and Scud-B missile systems would be removed. Some associated nuclear warheads would also be withdrawn. Finally, an unspecified number of air defense systems would be withdrawn, Nike-Hercules or Hawk by the United States and SAM-2 by the Soviet Union. The second phase would begin the following year, 1977, with a freeze on personnel and equipment by all parties; in 1978 all direct participants would cut their forces by some equal percentage to be negotiated as part of the initial agreement.

This proposal did not yield any ground on the issues of greatest concern to the West. It did not promise an outcome in which ground forces on the two sides would be equal in numbers; it still envisaged individual national ceilings for all the direct participants in the negotiations. On the other hand, there were new elements in this proposal. Previously the East had called for reduction of all types of weapons across the board, but now it specified types and numbers of military equipment—tanks, aircraft, missile and air defense systems. Also new was the acceptance of a two-phase reduction process beginning with the superpowers. There was no real meeting of the minds on this matter, however. NATO's two phases meant that only after a Phase I agree-

29

ment prescribing the reduction in U.S. and Soviet forces had been concluded would negotiation on the content of a Phase II agreement begin; the Warsaw Pact insisted that the reductions be agreed to by all parties at one time, after which the agreement would be implemented in two phases. One other new element in this Warsaw Pact proposal was that units withdrawn by the two major powers were to be disbanded, not simply moved elsewhere. Their personnel and equipment, however, could be added to existing units outside the reduction area.

A New NATO Offer Withheld

In October 1977, press reports indicated that a new proposal had been prepared by the NATO nations for presentation in Vienna.[5] This proposal, devised in its essential elements by the West Germans and transmitted to President Carter in July, would have modified somewhat the Western position on a first-phase Soviet reduction.

Throughout the negotiations, the West had demanded the withdrawal of a complete Soviet tank army. The NATO position was that the only Soviet unit whose withdrawal would meet its demand was the First Tank Army of the Guards, headquartered in Dresden, which —according to one German newspaper—is "the best in all the Soviet Armed Forces."[6] The new proposal approved by the NATO nations would permit the removal of any five Soviet tank divisions from the reduction area, rather than a specific, complete tank army. The new proposal would probably also reduce somewhat the number of tanks to be withdrawn and apparently would permit other equipment associated with these divisions to remain. This proposal would not change significantly the number of Soviet troops to be withdrawn, nor would it make any quantitative additions to the Western offer to reduce American forces and equipment.

The new offer was ready for presentation to the Warsaw Pact in December 1977, before the conclusion of the thirteenth round of the negotiations, but it was withheld by the West because of the collapse of efforts to resolve a conflict between the two sides on another issue—the number of ground troops the Pact presently stations in Central Europe. Presumably, the new NATO offer will be submitted in a later round of the negotiations.

---

[5] "Allies Ready Proposal on Troop Cuts," *New York Times*, October 25, 1977.
[6] *Die Welt*, November 1, 1977, p. 6.

30

The Issues Summarized

The two sides in the Vienna negotiations are presently in disagreement on eight distinct issues. Two of these are basic issues related to the overall outcome sought through the negotiations. Five can be regarded as secondary issues that relate to more limited aspects of the outcome or to procedures involved in the implementation of an agreement. The eighth issue, the head count of Warsaw Pact forces in the reduction area, is a question of fact and is the issue on which the talks were deadlocked in December 1977.

The two basic issues are *parity* and *collectivity*. Parity connotes the reduction of military personnel in Central Europe to an equal number on both sides. This outcome, NATO argues, should be expressly accepted in a first-phase agreement as the ultimate goal of the negotiations, and both sides should commit themselves to it in terms as specific as NATO's proposed ceiling of 700,000 ground troops or 900,000 ground and air troops combined. The Warsaw Pact nations have not been willing to endorse parity in military manpower as the goal, in either general or specific terms, but have clung to the position that each side should reduce its forces by equal numbers or equal percentages.

There is a deliberate ambiguity in the Warsaw Pact position on the question of parity. Figures the Pact supplied after the negotiations had been going on for more than two years indicate that Eastern air and ground forces in the reduction zone are about equal to those of the Western nations. This contradicts NATO's count which showed 150,000 more Eastern than Western troops in the area at the opening of the negotiations. The implication of the figures supplied by the East, of course, is that a reduction in equal numbers or equal percentages by both sides would maintain a parity that already exists. The corollary implication is that the unequal numerical reductions the West proposed would change the relationship of the two sides from parity to Western superiority. If NATO's head count of forces in Central Europe is accurate, however, applying the reduction formula proposed by the East would result in a permanent force disparity in favor of the Warsaw Pact.

On the second basic issue—collectivity—there is no element of ambiguity about the disagreement between the two sides. The Warsaw Pact insists upon specifying for each and every direct participant in the negotiations a ceiling on the manpower it can maintain in the reduction area. The West proposes a collective manpower ceiling applicable either to ground troops only or to ground and air force

31

personnel combined. Within this collective ceiling, individual nations other than the United States and the Soviet Union would be free to increase their military manpower. If, for example, after reductions to the collective ceiling had been made, the Netherlands and Belgium were to reduce their forces by 50,000 more, the Federal Republic of Germany could add 50,000 men to its forces. This is exactly the kind of situation which the Soviet Union wants to prevent. It is no secret that the Soviet Union and its allies insist on incorporating individual national troop celings in an agreement in order to establish an absolute limitation on the size of the West German Bundeswehr.

The remaining points of disagreement are not unimportant, but they should be more susceptible to compromise than the two primary issues. First is the question of what is to be reduced—a matter on which both sides have modified their original positions. NATO began with the principle that reductions would be limited to ground forces. Its original proposal for reductions of undesignated American ground force personnel and of one complete Soviet tank army was amended in 1975. The additions NATO then made to its offer of reductions were a mixed bag of U.S. tactical nuclear weapons, nuclear-capable aircraft, and surface-to-surface missiles.

By contrast, the Warsaw Pact initially proposed reductions going beyond ground manpower, embracing both air and ground personnel and extending to a great range of equipment and weapons, nuclear as well as conventional. The portion of its 1976 proposal that relates to the first phase of reductions on the part of the United States and the Soviet Union is less sweeping and specifies a limited number of weapons systems and equipment for reduction. There remains, however, a chasm to be bridged between the Western and the Eastern concepts about reductions in subsequent phases.

A second issue is the phasing of reductions. The Warsaw Pact has come around to acceptance of a part of the NATO concept—the execution of reductions in two steps, with the first step taken by the United States and the Soviet Union. But disagreement remains on a more fundamental question. The Western position calls for two separate force reduction agreements—one relating to the reductions to be undertaken by the United States and the Soviet Union alone and a second, to be negotiated subsequently, on further reductions on the part of all direct participants. The first-phase agreement would obligate all parties to enter on a second round of negotiation to bring troop levels down to a designated collective ceiling, but it would not guarantee a second round agreement. As 1977 ended, the West had gone no further than to offer to commence negotiations on a second

32

phase of reductions within eighteen months after the conclusion of an agreement on first-phase cuts and to state that all participants will reduce their forces in the second phase.

The Eastern position, as explained by a Warsaw Pact spokesman to the press, is that in a first-phase agreement each of the direct participants in the negotiations should "state the approximate date and volume of their reductions in the second stage."[7] The difference, then, between the two sides is this: NATO proposes to negotiate in two phases; the Warsaw Pact proposes to execute reductions in two phases but to settle all the significant issues in one.

A third point of disagreement concerns offers both sides have made for a freeze on existing troop levels in the reduction area. In 1974 the Western nations sought to meet a Communist objection to their concept of negotiation in two phases by offering to pledge not to increase NATO forces in the reduction area after a first-phase agreement had been concluded. The Warsaw Pact counterproposal called for a declaration not to increase then existing force levels rather than waiting for the conclusion of an agreement.

In addition to the difference under the two proposals as to when a freeze on force levels should go into effect, the disagreement on whether the ceiling should be collective or national again arose in connection with these proposals. The freeze on force levels intended by the NATO nations would be a collective ceiling whereas the freeze proposed by the Warsaw Pact would impose individual national manpower ceilings on each of the direct participants.

A fourth issue, which can be regarded as secondary if only because it has not so far been sharply defined, is the question of verification. NATO in its MBFR guidelines promulgated in Rome in 1970 stressed the importance of including as part of any force reduction agreement "adequate verification and controls" to prevent cheating. The Western nations tried to introduce the subject in the negotiations, but the Pact nations have refused to discuss the matter until "issues of principle" have been resolved. If and when verification becomes a subject of negotiation, disagreement between the two sides on this subject can be anticipated. It is likely that the Warsaw Pact powers will accept no more than minimal measures and will reject any intrusive controls, and it is far from clear how far NATO—particularly the

---

[7] Press conference statement of Polish Ambassador Slawomir Dabrowa, July 21, 1976. This softened Dabrowa's earlier demand in a press conference of January 30, 1976, that in conjunction with a first-phase reduction agreement "each of the direct participants must unequivocally and precisely specify what, when, and how it is going to reduce."

Federal Republic of Germany—is prepared to go toward accepting controls involving the presence of Pact inspectors on Western territory.

A fifth issue, temporarily resolved in the preparatory talks, relates to the extent of the reduction area, specifically whether Hungary is to be included within it. When NATO argued early on for the inclusion of Hungary, the Soviet Union countered that it would propose the inclusion of Italy in the reduction area. This prospect weakened NATO's solidarity on the question, upsetting Italy and the other indirect participants along the Mediterranean. In the preparatory talks, agreement was reached to exclude Hungary from the reduction area provisionally but to defer final settlement of the issue. It is not likely that the West will renew the fight on this matter, but technically the issue awaits final resolution.

Finally, there is the issue of the size of Warsaw Pact forces in the reduction area of Central Europe. NATO provided a count of the ground forces on both sides in 1974. The Warsaw Pact offered a count of its ground and air force personnel in early 1976. Late in the year, NATO provided an updated tally of its manpower in the area.

Table 1 compares the ground force strength of the two sides in the reduction area as estimated by NATO in 1973 and 1976 and presents the strength reported by the Warsaw Pact nations for their side in the latter year. Compared with NATO's calculations at the beginning of negotiations in 1973, its figures computed in 1976 show an increase of 37,000 for Warsaw Pact ground forces and an increase of 21,000 in Western ground forces.[8] When air force personnel are added to the most recent figures in Table 1, the gap between the calculations by the two sides remains. According to NATO, each side has approximately 200,000 air force personnel in the area, which would make the combined totals 1,162,000 for the East and 991,000 for the West. According to *Pravda*, the totals rise to 987,300 for the East and 981,000 for the West, reducing the difference between the two to a mere 6,300.[9]

During the entire year of 1977, the problem of reconciling the conflicting figures on the size of the Warsaw Pact forces in Central

---

[8] A NATO spokesman told the press in Vienna on April 19, 1978, that this increase "did not represent an increase of the forces but rather was the consequence of refined computation." Press Conference of Ambassador Willem de Vos van Steenwijk of the Netherlands.

[9] The figures reported by each side for its own forces in 1976 were given in *Pravda* on June 8, 1977, in an article captioned "Vienna Talks: Why Has There Been No Progress?" *FBIS Daily Report, Soviet Union*, June 10, 1977. The figures NATO provided in 1973 have been widely published; see, for example, *New York Times*, December 13, 1973.

34

TABLE 1

NATO AND WARSAW PACT ESTIMATES OF GROUND FORCE MANPOWER IN THE CENTRAL REGION, 1973 AND 1976

Source	Pact	NATO	Disparity
1973 NATO estimates	925,000	770,000	155,000
1976 NATO estimates	962,000	791,000	171,000
1976 Warsaw Pact report	805,000	—[a]	14,000[b]

[a] Not specified.
[b] Difference between figures submitted in 1976 by each side for its own forces.

Europe dominated the negotiations. Seeking to resolve the disagreement, the West asked the Pact for a breakdown of aggregate figures for ground forces so that the discrepancy between the two conflicting estimates could be identified in terms of force elements. For a time in late 1977, the Western delegations expressed hope that a breakdown of the Eastern force total would be supplied in this form. The Pact, however, was unwilling to comply with the Western request unless the West pledged in advance to raise no further questions about the count of Eastern forces and to accept whatever figures were submitted as accurate. This was the impasse in which the negotiators found themselves when they ended their thirteenth round of talks on December 15, 1977.

Manpower and Tank Comparisons

In the Vienna negotiations, the NATO nations have focused on two elements of the military balance in which they perceive Soviet superiority—manpower and tanks. Table 2 compares NATO and Warsaw Pact strength in Central Europe in these two forces. These figures show a disparity favoring the Warsaw Pact in both tanks and manpower of the same magnitude as NATO's figures reflect.

Individual national contributions to the total forces on the two sides present an interesting contrast. Fifty percent of the Warsaw Pact ground forces are Soviet soldiers whereas American troops make up only 25 percent of NATO's ground forces. Soviet troops make up more than 75 percent of Pact ground forces stationed in East Germany. West Germany is the leading national contingent on the

35

TABLE 2

Comparison of Elements of NATO and Warsaw Pact Strength in Central Europe, 1977

Country	Manpower (in thousands)		Tanks
	Ground	Air	
NATO			
United States	193	35	2,000
Britain	58	9	575
Canada	3	2	30
Belgium	62	19	300
Germany	341	110	3,000
Netherlands	75	18	500
Subtotal	732	193	6,405
France	50	0	325
Total	782	193	6,730
Warsaw Pact			
Soviet Union	475	60	9,250
Czechoslovakia	135	46	2,500
East Germany	105	36	1,550
Poland	220	62	2,900
Total	935	204	16,200

Source: *The Military Balance, 1977–78* (London: International Institute for Strategic Studies), p. 110.

Western side; it provides about 45 percent of the total NATO manpower and more than 50 percent of the air force personnel.

Over the course of the past fifteen years, the aggregate number of NATO ground forces in Central Europe has not changed greatly. A change has occurred, however, in the relative contributions of the individual nations to the total. All except Germany have reduced their forces to some degree, but the German increase has offset the reductions of the other nations. In 1962, the United States and Germany each accounted for about one-third of Western ground force strength in the area. Currently, as we have seen, German troops constitute 45 percent of the total, and American forces, about 25 percent.

The Warsaw Pact ground forces have increased, most significantly in 1968. Soviet divisions in the proposed reduction area of Central Europe were increased at that time from twenty-two to twenty-seven, five of which are stationed in Czechoslovakia, and they have been kept at that level since 1968.

A count of Soviet divisions that ignores actual strength at any given time and is limited to the reduction area can be misleading. Comparable historical figures are not available to provide precise measurement of the growth of Soviet ground forces in Central Europe since 1968. Defense Department estimates, however, do indicate the change in the size of Russian military forces of all branches stationed in Europe outside the Soviet Union. They show an increase from 415,000 in 1967 and 480,000 in 1968 to 575,000 at the end of 1973. Over the same period 1967–1973, U. S. forces of all branches stationed in Europe declined from 337,000 to 300,000.

The Basic Issue: Military Balance in Central Europe

Both sides went to Vienna ostensibly to seek agreement on force reductions, but with clashing concepts of the desired outcome. NATO wished not only to reduce forces but to change the existing relationship between the military strength of the two sides in Central Europe. The Warsaw Pact wished to reduce force levels but to maintain their existing relationship. At the very opening of substantive negotiations, on November 5, 1973, Polish Ambassador Tadeusz Strulak told the press:

> The realistic approach to the problem of mutual reduction of forces and armaments in Central Europe requires that it should be carried out with due respect to the existing relationship of forces, which satisfies the objective needs of European security. Our understanding of the principle of undiminished security is that, while lowering the level of forces and armaments, this relationship of forces should be maintained.[10]

This fundamental disagreement was what the argument in the preparatory talks over the use of the word "balanced" in describing the subject matter of the negotiations was all about.

---

[10] In a similar vein, Brezhnev, speaking to the World Peace Congress in Moscow on October 25, 1973, said, "It is important that the future reduction should not upset the existing balance of strength in Central Europe and in the European continent generally. If there are attempts to violate this principle, the entire issue will only become an apple of discord and the subject of endless debate." *New York Times*, October 27, 1973.

37

The West contended that the Warsaw Pact possessed a substantial margin of superiority in Central Europe, particularly in ground force manpower and tanks. The East contended initially that, all things considered, the existing relation between forces was one of balance. Eventually they added to this thesis the argument that, even with regard to military manpower, there was approximate parity.

On June 8, 1977, *Pravda* restated the Warsaw Pact view on this basic issue of the Vienna negotiations:

> The task is to reduce the high level of concentration of troops and armaments in this region *without infringing upon the existing balance of forces*. [Italics added.] For this reason the adoption of equal percentage reductions has been proposed as a basis for an agreement.

As for the NATO reduction proposals, *Pravda* continued:

> There is no element of any reciprocity or equality in reductions here. . . . There are direct attempts to alter the balance of forces in central Europe to the unilateral advantage of the Western countries and to the detriment of the interests of the security of the socialist countries. The Soviet Union and its allies naturally cannot and will not agree to this.

The Western force reduction proposal, designed to rectify the imbalances of greatest concern to NATO, is asymmetrical in its terms, imposing greater restraints on the Soviet Union than on the United States. NATO's rationale for setting more rigorous requirements for the Soviet Union rests on the fact that Russia enjoys two types of advantages in the exercise of military power in Central Europe. One advantage lies in the preponderance of manpower and certain types of weapons and equipment the Soviet Union and its allies station in the region. The second advantage is geographical. The Soviet Union, adjoining the reduction area and only 600 kilometers from the frontier of West Germany, can return withdrawn forces with a speed which the United States, 6,000 kilometers away, cannot match.

To compensate for these advantages, the Western proposal begins with a commitment that requires a manpower reduction on the Warsaw Pact side that is almost three times that required in NATO forces. Thus the disparity in military manpower would be eliminated. A second disparity exists in the number of tanks in the region. According to NATO's count in 1973, Pact tanks in the area outnumbered Western tanks by 9,500. This disparity would be reduced, although not eliminated, by the requirement that 1,700 Soviet tanks be withdrawn without requiring the removal of a single tank on the NATO side. Tanks were specified rather than other types of weapons systems in which the Communist states have superiority because, in the minds of NATO strategists, the firepower and mobility of tanks make them the most important and threatening offensive type of weapon, particularly for a blitzkrieg-style attack with minimum advance warning.

The requirement in the Western proposal that only the Soviet Union withdraw all arms and equipment associated with troops removed from Central Europe was intended to compensate for the geographical advantage which the Soviet Union, next door neighbor to Central Europe, possesses in comparison with the remote United States. If the arms and equipment of the withdrawn American forces remained in Central Europe pre-positioned and ready for use in the event that the forces returned, a rapid rebuilding of military strength lost in the reduction process would be possible. Men can be moved quickly by air whereas the movement of substantial quantities of heavy military equipment, relying primarily on sea and land transport, is slow.

By any standard, the initial Western offer at Vienna was too one-sided to be enticing to the East. To sweeten the proposal and break the two-year deadlock in the negotiations, Option III, the additional U.S. proposal to withdraw specific Western weapons, was argued out in NATO and offered in December 1975. The Western side reasoned that an offer to withdraw elements of a weapons system which the East professed to regard as threatening might strike the Warsaw Pact as a reasonable exchange for withdrawal of a considerable number of tanks. There could be little doubt that the Communist world, which had proposed the Rapacki plan for a denuclearized zone and had for twenty years vehemently protested the Western nuclear arsenal in Central Europe, placed high priority on removing nuclear weapons from the area. By proposing to cut down on such weapons and by indicating willingness to limit air force personnel, the West abandoned its initial position that its reductions should be confined to ground force manpower. It took a step in the direction of the Eastern position that anything military in the area should be fair game for reduction.

Apparently, there was a belief in Washington, encouraged by both Soviet and other diplomatic personnel, that the new Western proposal would break the logjam and lead to agreement. A "high-ranking Ford administration official" told the *New York Times* that a proposal to withdraw about 1,000 nuclear weapons from Western Europe "would lead to 'a breakthrough' . . . enabling the Soviet

39

Union to comply with the Western demand that it withdraw a tank army from East Germany."[11]

The value of Option III as a bargaining chip was severely discounted, however, by numerous published reports earlier in 1975 that much of the tactical nuclear arsenal maintained by the United States was obsolescent, that more effective "mini-nucs" were in development, and that the United States did not know what to do with the 7,000 tactical nuclear warheads it had stocked in Europe. It was hardly a secret that U.S. authorities had considered withdrawing part of its nuclear weapons from Europe, independently of the Vienna negotiations.[12] The Warsaw Pact nations may have suspected that the concession offered in Option III was something that would come to pass whether or not they signed a force reduction agreement.

Divergent Western Views on Balanced Forces in Central Europe

Some have questioned the value of establishing a balance within Central Europe because it is so restricted an area and because it adjoins the Soviet Union. In the early stages of NATO's study of the matter of force reductions, a majority of its MBFR Working Group initially favored including a substantially greater part of Europe in the reduction area. When Central Europe was accepted as the area of reduction, some members of the group still sought to stretch it to include the three westernmost districts of the Soviet Union.

Italy, Greece, and Turkey are among those who remain skeptical about the usefulness of any agreement that cuts Soviet forces in the reduction area but permits them to be shifted to Hungary or to other parts of Eastern Europe or within the Soviet Union closer to NATO's southern flank along the Mediterranean. Various noncircumvention measures to avoid such an outcome have been considered by the Western alliance, and the nature and extent of noncircumvention restrictions will emerge as a difficult issue to resolve, if the negotiations reach that stage.

It is true that a better balance of forces within Central Europe

---

[11] "U.S. Gets Favorable Hints," *New York Times*, December 13, 1975.

[12] The *New York Times* of July 24, 1975, for example, in an article captioned "U.S. Delaying Removal of Warheads," reported that the Defense Department regarded its stockpile of 7,000 nuclear warheads in Western Europe as "too large for military requirements and composed of too many obsolete weapons." The story said the Defense Department had presented to President Ford a plan to reduce the warheads but that the State Department wanted to use them "as a bargaining chip to prevail upon the Warsaw Pact nations to reduce their conventional forces . . ."

40

alone may not reduce military risks for the NATO nations. The disposition of withdrawn Russian forces may pose an increased threat to the states on NATO's flanks. Or the capacity of the West for timely reinforcement in Central Europe might be degraded in comparison to that of the Warsaw Pact, particularly insofar as Western reinforcement involves returning troops pulled back across the Atlantic. Nevertheless, an agreement limited to force reductions in Central Europe could have considerable value to the West if its effect were to diminish the capacity of the East for sudden massive attack and if collateral measures to reduce risks were adopted.

A broader question to which the conflicting claims of the two sides at Vienna invite attention is whether, all things considered, a military imbalance does in fact exist in Central Europe. The underlying rationale of the proposals made by the Warsaw Pact is that an overall balance does exist which should be preserved by symmetrical reductions of comparable forces by the two sides.

An impartial and informed source based in London, the International Institute of Strategic Studies, summarizes its appraisal of the current military balance between NATO and Warsaw Pact forces in Central Europe in these words:

> A balance between NATO and the Warsaw Pact cannot be struck by a mere comparison of manpower, combat units or equipment. In the first place, the Pact has numerical superiority by some measures, and NATO by others, and there is no fully satisfactory way to compare these asymmetrical advantages. Secondly, qualitative factors that cannot be reduced to numbers, such as training, morale, leadership, tactical initiative and geographical positions could prove dominant in warfare. However, three observations can be made by way of summary:

> First, the overall balance is such as to make military aggression appear unattractive. The defenses are of such a size and quality that any attempt to breach them would require major attack. The consequences for an attacker would be incalculable, and the risks, including that of nuclear escalation, must impose caution. . . .

> Second, NATO has emphasized quality, particularly in equipment and training, to offset numbers, but this is in danger of erosion. New technology has strengthened the defence, but it will become increasingly expensive in the future. If defence budgets in the West are maintained no higher than their present level and manpower costs continue to rise, the

Warsaw Pact may be able to buy more of the new systems than NATO. Soviet spending has been increasing steadily, in real terms, for many years. Furthermore, technology cannot be counted on to offset numerical advantages entirely.

Thirdly, while an overall balance can be said to exist today, the Warsaw Pact apears more content with it than NATO.[13]

During the early phases of the force reduction negotiations, American defense spokesmen also tended to assess the balance of forces in Europe in relatively reassuring terms, emphasizing such factors as the qualitative superiority of the West and the length of the mobilization period the East would require before it could be prepared to launch a major attack.[14] Now, however, these optimistic appraisals seem to be giving way to expressions of heightened concern about recent trends in the relationship of forces.

Current Pentagon thinking presumably is reflected in testimony given by Ambassador Robert W. Komer, adviser to the secretary of defense on NATO affairs, to a congressional committee in October 1977:

The conventional balance in Europe—while not badly tilted against NATO—is more precarious than it should be. While the Pact cannot be confident of breaking through NATO's forward defenses, NATO cannot be confident of preventing a major breakthrough. Moreover, the trend is worrisome—unless NATO pulls up its socks. . . . We are sufficiently uncomfortable about the conventional NATO/Warsaw Pact balance, and the growth in Warsaw Pact capabilities, that we and our allies believe a major effort to improve NATO's own defense posture is imperative.[15]

John Collins, senior specialist in national defense in the Congressional Research Service of the Library of Congress, concludes

---

[13] *The Military Balance, 1977–1978* (London: International Institute for Strategic Studies, 1977).

[14] The appraisals of the military balance expressed by successive secretaries of defense since the time of Robert McNamara have tended to follow lines set out in Alain C. Enthoven and K. Wayne Smith, *How Much Is Enough?* (New York: Harper, 1971). See, for example, Secretary of Defense James Schlesinger's statement to Congress, U.S. Senate Armed Services Committee, *Hearings on the FY 1976 Defense Budget* (Washington, 1975), pp. 321–22. An excellent analysis is in Robert L. Fischer, *Defending the Central Front: The Balance of Forces*, Adelphi Paper 127 (London: International Institute for Strategic Studies, 1976).

[15] Statement of Robert W. Komer before the Europe and Middle East Subcommittee of the Committee on International Relations, U.S. House of Representatives, October 3, 1977.

42

an exhaustive comparison of the forces of the two sides with a more alarming judgment:

> Emerging Soviet capabilities, with great stress on offensive shock power, create a new strategic environment. . . . Consequently, the overall balance has not been so lopsided since the early 1950's, before NATO's bulwark was completed.[16]

Nongovernmental organizations, such as the Committee on the Present Danger and the Atlantic Council, have echoed the concern about the shift in the balance in favor of the East. NATO military authorities have tended consistently to take a highly pessimistic view of the balance of forces, an appraisal reflected in most public pronouncements of the alliance. Retired Belgian General Robert Close, in a book written while serving as director of studies at the NATO Defense College in Rome, concludes that "the crushing Soviet superiority resulting from constant qualitative and quantitative improvements is destroying the balance of forces" in Europe. General Close describes how the Warsaw Pact could by sudden overpowering attack move across the Rhine in three places within forty-eight hours.[17]

Acceptance of the belief that Soviet military capability in Europe has grown in recent years at a pace unmatched by the West has had a marked effect on attitudes within the Congress as well as in the Department of Defense. Resistance to increases in the defense budget has waned, and proposals to reduce American troop strength in Europe are no longer heard on Capitol Hill.

A word of caution is in order about estimates of the military balance and about dynamic analyses of hypothetical conflict situations between opposing military forces. They are flawed to some degree by the imprecision and the uncertainty that cloud many factors in the analyses. A series of assumptions must be made that are crucial to the hypothetical outcome of postulated military engagements. If the assumptions are not realized in a real life situation, the actual outcome can be far different from that of the theoretical model.

In NATO's defense planning, the most crucial assumption relates to the amount of warning time the West would have in which to get ready to meet a major attack from the East. In the past, some have held the belief that such an attack would require a long period of

---

[16] John Collins, "American and Soviet Military Strength, Contemporary Trends Compared 1970–1976," *Congressional Record*, August 5, 1977, pp. S14064–14104.

[17] Robert Close, *L'Europe sans Défense?* (Brussels: Collections Inédits, 1976), chaps. 9 and 10.

large-scale, detectable preparations by the Warsaw Pact and that within a few days after the start of such activities NATO would have interpreted them as foretelling an assault and would start to reinforce its defenses. If this assumption about the amount of warning time the West could expect is accurate, there is ground for reasonable confidence in NATO's ability to defend successfully. But, if the warning time is shortened and/or the time the West takes to reach decisions and take action is lengthened, doubt mounts about the outcome. It is worth noting that Ambassador Komer, testifying as the representative of the Defense Department, did not encourage the Congress to expect that the West would have a very long warning of attack. His estimate of warning time was "at the very least a few days and probably more" if the Warsaw Pact were to decide "to mount a truly meaningful attack."[18]

Is Disparity in Manpower the Problem?

Recently, both in the United States and in Europe, several authorities have defined the great military problem confronting the West in Central Europe as the capability of the Warsaw Pact for a sudden overwhelming attack which NATO could not meet in timely fashion. A report by Senators Sam Nunn of Georgia and Dewey Bartlett of Oklahoma on January 24, 1977, brought to public attention the misgivings within the U.S. government about accepted assumptions on the warning time that might be expected to precede a Communist attack on Western Europe.[19]

The Nunn-Bartlett report asserted, "The manpower disparities between NATO and the Warsaw Pact in the designated reduction area . . . are not the major NATO problem." Rather, the serious disparity is one of readiness on the two sides.

> The Soviets have provided their . . . forces deployed opposite West Germany an ability to initiate a potentially devastating invasion of Europe with as little as a few days warning. This is evident in a growing emphasis upon firepower and readiness of ground forces and in the dramatic transformation of Soviet tactical aviation from a defensive force into a hard-hitting offensive air armada of extended reach.

[18] Komer, statement before Europe and Middle East Subcommittee, Committee on International Relations.
[19] "NATO and the New Soviet Threat," *Congressional Record*, January 25, 1977, pp. S1411–1417.

44

While Soviet forces in Eastern Europe can initiate a conflict from virtually a standing start, NATO forces continue to require warning time of a duration sufficient to permit the Alliance to mobilize and deploy to the center of conflict its ultimately greater but typically less ready and poorly deployed forces.

Consequently, the report concludes, NATO's real worry is not superior numbers of Pact manpower but "superiority in firepower, greater readiness, and unsurpassed mobility."

This view of the danger in Central Europe led the two senators to recommend that NATO should seek in the Vienna talks "to reduce Soviet firepower in the . . . area, to provide the necessary verification means to insure that it is not reintroduced, and to take steps which would improve early warning of impending attack."

Senators Nunn and Bartlett and others who share their views are suggesting a reorientation of the Western approach to the negotiations in Vienna which would relegate manpower reductions to a secondary place on the agenda. Senator Nunn, in a speech delivered on November 14, 1977, explicitly called for such a reorientation:

> I believe that the ongoing Soviet military buildup in Eastern Europe dictates a shift in our focus at MBFR from seeking a reduction in the aggregate number of Warsaw Pact troops in Central Europe to that of increasing NATO's warning time. This means focusing on obtaining removal of forward-deployed Soviet combat units as units, together with all their equipment, including artillery and armored personnel carriers—not just tanks. It means focusing on a more readily verifiable agreement. There are undoubtedly other feasible confidence-building measures which would increase warning time, but an important political decision first must be made by NATO to change the focus and direction at MBFR.[20]

As time goes by, a new approach of this kind may come to be regarded by the NATO nations as the best way to seek to maintain their security.

---

[20] "Mutual and Balanced Force Reductions—A Need to Shift our Focus," speech prepared for delivery before the Georgia Chamber of Commerce, Augusta, Georgia, November 14, 1977.

3

The Process of Negotiating: Washington, Brussels, and Vienna

The negotiating process in connection with the force reduction talks is unusually complex in that it involves three different forums. One forum is within the U.S. government, where negotiation takes place among the agencies that participate in making foreign and defense policy decisions. A second is in NATO, where negotiation goes on with our allies. Agreement in Brussels leads to the third forum in Vienna, where NATO negotiates with the Warsaw Pact.

The procedure is cumbersome; it is not designed for speedy decision making. Nine months elapsed before Option III cleared the gauntlet through which it had to pass in Brussels before it could be offered to the East in Vienna in mid-December 1975. The procedure also is weighted toward compromise, least-common-denominator positions. NATO is, after all, an alliance of equal sovereign nations, and the need to recognize and resolve differing views and divergent interests makes compromises the normal product of the machinery. Before NATO can speak or act, a consensus must be arrived at within the alliance. A consensus does not require unanimous agreement, but, to achieve consensus, any nations which disagree must either remove themselves from participation in the decision or remain mute.

In Vienna the negotiations are bilateral. There, the parties are the two rival military alliances, not their constituent countries. Although the Communist view is that the talks are not "bloc to bloc" negotiations, the behavior of the Eastern nations does not jibe with this theory. No individual nation on either side in the negotiations proper has expressed a view or submitted a proposal that was not supported by the other participants on its side. At formal conference meetings and in formal dealings with the press, a single spokesman

47

appears from each side. The process by which NATO positions are formed is well known, and these positions require the approval of the NATO council. A veil shrouds the process on the Eastern side, but there is always complete solidarity among the Pact members on all matters and no expression of dissent.

The Apparatus in Washington

The players in Washington who participate in deliberations relating to the force reduction talks represent the following: in the Defense Department, the Office of the Secretary and the Joint Chiefs of Staff; in the State Department, the European Bureau and the Politico-Military Bureau; the Arms Control and Disarmament Agency; the National Security Council; and the intelligence community.

Despite some initial aversion, especially within the Defense Department, to entering negotiations considered unlikely to yield an agreement advantageous to the West, MBFR talks were accepted by all as politically necessary and by some as desirable. In formulating negotiating positions, disagreements within the United States government seem not to have been numerous, basic, or bitter. That harmony may not continue is suggested by some recent developments. There were critical reactions to the impending new NATO offer, worked out in the latter half of 1977, on the withdrawal of Soviet tank forces.[1] Further, press reports of a mid-November 1977 National Security Council meeting to decide whether to add to the West's outstanding offer a pledge not to deploy neutron weapons in the reduction area indicated sharp division within the government on this question.[2]

Although force reduction issues have commanded continuing serious attention of able staff and have generated their fair share of the paper flow within government, they seem to have had rather limited consideration at high policy-making levels. Top decision makers have been preoccupied with strategic arms limitations problems in the belief that no progress is likely in Vienna until a new SALT agreement has

---

[1] The new offer which the West had ready for presentation in Vienna after approval by the NATO Permanent Representatives on December 5, 1977, was sharply criticized by Senator Sam Nunn in a speech before the Georgia Chamber of Commerce, Augusta, Georgia, November 14, 1977, entitled "Mutual and Balanced Force Reductions—A Need to Shift Our Forces."

[2] "Backers of Neutron Arms Win Round," *Washington Post*, November 23, 1977; "U.S. May Offer Soviet Deal Shelving Neutron Bomb," *New York Times*, November 24, 1977.

48

been concluded. Thus, force reduction negotiations have been kept on a back burner.

Interesting as it might be to trace the process of negotiation within the U.S. government leading up to the submission of MBFR proposals for consideration by our NATO allies, this subject cannot yet be treated in an unclassified publication. Further, the distinctive aspect of MBFR negotiations lies in the fact that they involve an alliance and that hammering out a negotiating position requires agreement among many nations. How the problems related to MBFR were handled in Brussels is the part of the process that merits particular attention.

Negotiation within NATO

In 1968, studies began in the NATO bureaucracy looking toward negotiations with the East on force reductions.[3] The pace was leisurely, and the work went forward without noticeable display of interest or enthusiasm. In 1970, in a move to upgrade the process, the Permanent Representatives to NATO called on the Military Committee of the alliance to provide a study and appropriate recommendations on mutual force reduction. The response showed that there was still little interest in the subject. The Military Committee, pleading that it lacked the required staff resources, proposed that the task be given to an ad hoc group of special representatives selected by the various member nations from the ranks of their own civil servants.

Thus the MBFR Working Group—the agency that amassed the information and provided the recommendations from which NATO's negotiating positions were developed—came into being. In order to find a chairman for the Working Group, it was necessary to resort to drafting the deputy chairman of NATO's Military Committee, an American air force general, for the post.

In mid-1971 the lethargy that characterized NATO's initial approach to MBFR concerns was replaced by a more serious mood and greater activity. Coincidentally with the struggle in the Senate over the Mansfield resolution, the United States began to show interest in the subject. Lieutenant General Edward L. Rowny, U.S.A., newly arrived deputy chairman of the NATO Military Committee, quickened the pace of the MBFR Working Group.

---

[3] The information in this section was gathered largely by personal interviews in Brussels, Vienna, and Washington with participants in, and observers of, the events.

49

Washington's changed attitude, demonstrated in such ways as dispatching experts from the Pentagon and the State Department to Brussels to consult on force reduction, prompted a response within NATO. Experts began arriving from London and Bonn. The membership of the MBFR Working Group was enlarged, and the group began to meet with greater regularity.

Further evidence that MBFR was becoming a subject of importance within NATO appeared when bureaucratic rivalry for jurisdiction over the subject emerged between the military and the political agencies of the alliance. Originally spurned by the Military Committee and entrusted to the ad hoc Working Group, the problems of staking out the Western position on mutual force reductions now attracted the interest of NATO's Senior Political Committee.

The disagreements between the military and political experts were sometimes difficult to resolve. The MBFR Working Group, reflecting a military orientation, was more concerned about avoiding risk to Western security than about promoting détente or making the Western bargaining position acceptable to the East. The Senior Political Committee, on the other hand, was more interested in staking out a Western position that carried some hope of leading to an agreement with the East and was more ready to accept a modest element of risk in connection with a mutual reduction of forces.

It was not until mid-1973 that NATO positions on all major issues relating to the MBFR negotiations were firmly established. The unity which the West was to exhibit in the negotiations at Vienna did not come easily in all cases. The major issues battled out in NATO agencies were the questions of the geographical area of reduction, the forces to be considered candidates for reduction, the related issue of what troops to count in determining a base from which reductions would be made, and the scale of reductions to be sought.

Although public declarations made both by NATO and by the Warsaw Pact seemed to point toward Central Europe alone as the area of reduction, initially some members of the MBFR Working Group preferred to expand the area. In the members' minds, a withdrawal of Russian forces from Central Europe only would not move them far enough from NATO's front lines to compensate for a removal of American forces from Europe.

The United Kingdom argued that the reduction area should include the three western districts of the Soviet Union in order to put a decent distance between any removed Soviet forces and the West. Other members of the Working Group could see no hope of persuading the Soviet Union to include any part of its own territory in the reduction zone unless the zone's western boundary were extended to some point in the United States. In time, the group was persuaded that the zone of reduction must be restricted and that Central Europe must be its heart.

The question of whether Hungary should be included in the reduction zone was also difficult to resolve. The Soviet Union permanently stations 60,000 troops in Hungary, and Hungary lies as close to West Germany as many areas of Poland. The United States argued that Hungary should be included, and—with greater fervor— so did the United Kingdom and the nations on NATO's southern flank. It was Italy, however, that felt most uneasy about the possible use of Hungarian territory as a base of attack. Because West Germany and the Benelux countries, the countries most affected by a reduction agreement, were less concerned whether Hungary was brought in or left out, the MBFR Working Group eventually leaned toward the exclusion of Hungary. Although this view did not prevail in setting the NATO position, it has been accepted at least tentatively by the negotiators in Vienna.

Although some people would have preferred to restrict the zone of reduction on the Western side to West Germany, such a proposal would have run into determined opposition from the Germans. One point on which Bonn had long been adamant was that it would not be singled out as the only Western nation with territory in the reduction zone. In deference to this stand, the Benelux countries offered their territory as part of the reduction zone to be proposed by NATO. Thus, the force reduction negotiations brought about a strange concept of Central Europe, stretching it to include some of the westernmost reaches of the continent.

Solving the problems of which reduction zone forces to count and which to reduce provoked serious differences of opinion among the experts in the MBFR Working Group. Agreement was reached at an early stage that reductions should be confined to ground forces. In a surprising twist, there was some sentiment to exclude the forces of the United States and the Soviet Union from the calculation of strength on both sides, as well as from reductions—a position that would have sent a good number of United States senators right through the Capitol's dome. Another suggestion was that a distinction be made between that part of Soviet forces stationed in Eastern European countries for occupation purposes and the part there for possible military action against the West and that reductions should

51

be taken only from the latter. The decision that was reached was to count all ground forces on both sides that were located within the area of reduction, regardless of nationality (including the French), and to refrain from excluding any (except the French) from a reduction agreement.

The MBFR Working Group settled on a preliminary count of ground forces that was reasonably close to the figures for Western troops which the NATO nations were to offer later at Vienna but that was below the final NATO figure for the East by approximately 50,000.

On the issue of symmetrical versus asymmetrical reductions, the majority of the members of the MBFR Working Group was clearly for the latter and for establishing a common troop ceiling for both sides at the completion of the reduction process. A minority of the members argued for an equal percentage reduction formula. In their opinion, the Soviet Union would agree to no other basis of reduction and would be unwilling to accept a reduction of more than 10 percent in the Warsaw Pact forces.

The principles on which NATO's proposals at Vienna were based were developed in Brussels through a process in which several nations affected the outcome. It was far from a one-nation show. The United States, the United Kingdom, the Federal Republic of Germany, some of the smaller nations, and even France, to a degree, contributed to the shaping of the NATO position in the MBFR Working Group.

When it came to designing the precise proposals that NATO was to submit at Vienna, however, the United States played a more assertive role. Until late 1977, the proposals were all developed in Washington and assented to by our allies in NATO. The initial MBFR proposal was accepted without a struggle by our allies. Option III, however, which departed from the principle that reductions would be confined to ground force manpower, caused our allies some anguish and aroused doubts and opposition. To secure the approval of NATO for Option III, Secretary Kissinger was forced to appeal to the other foreign ministers of the alliance at their meeting in December 1975.

As this instance indicates, the foreign ministers of the alliance nations constitute NATO's court of last resort. In ordinary circumstances, however, the ambassadors of the nations to NATO serve as both the decision makers and the watchdogs of the alliance in regard to the force reduction negotiations. They are kept fully informed of the proceedings in Vienna by their own on-the-spot representative and by a periodic exchange of information and views with representatives of the negotiating team who travel from Vienna to Brussels for that purpose.

52

National Roles and Attitudes

France is the only NATO nation which has taken a position opposing the MBFR negotiations.[4] France had withdrawn from the alliance's defense system in 1966, and it was not a party to the invitations to the Warsaw Pact to negotiate nor to NATO's earlier statements of principles governing an MBFR agreement nor to the pledge not to reduce combat capability except in the context of an agreement with the East on mutual force reductions. France, however, has not been loathe to express the view that the Vienna negotiations are an ill-advised exercise for the West. French spokesmen believe that any force reduction agreement that can be concluded will result in weakening NATO in relation to the Warsaw Pact and, consequently, will diminish the security of France.

Although not a participant in the NATO agencies that direct the alliance's integrated defense program, France has been an active and interested observer and one that is not without influence in staking out the positions taken by NATO on major MBFR issues. France also busied itself in fueling the opposition within the alliance to the Option III proposal of the United States.

Since France maintained a force of 60,000 men in Germany when the negotiations opened, the French attitude toward the talks has been awkward for the West. Paris has made it clear that it will not be bound by any agreement reached in Vienna. In 1976, when the West submitted to the Warsaw Pact updated figures on its troop strength in the reduction area, France objected to inclusion of its forces in the count, although it had permitted NATO to include its troops in the figure given to the Pact in 1974. In mid-1977, in contrast to the policy of the Western nations involved in the negotiations to maintain force levels in Germany, France announced its intention to reduce its force there by 10,000.

There is confidence among the other Western nations that France's abstention from the talks and its somewhat quixotic behavior are not obstacles to an MBFR agreement. The representatives of the West seem to believe that a common manpower ceiling, if one were agreed on in Vienna, would implicitly cover French forces. Then other Western nations would either have to negotiate with Paris to bring about an appropriate reduction of French forces or would have to

---

[4] French policy and its rationale are discussed in Michel Debré, "Défense de l'Europe et Securité en Europe," *Revue de Défense Nationale* (December 1972), pp. 1779-1804; and François de Rose, *La France et la Défense de l'Europe* (Paris: Seuil, 1976).

make further reductions in their own forces to the extent required to bring total Western forces below the ceiling. If this should come to pass, the diplomatic skills of the Western nations might be severely tested.

The NATO nations other than France are united in their quest for a force reduction agreement, but there are differences of attitude among them. Some are more eager than others to reach an agreement; some would be content to let the talks drift on inconclusively. Some are more concerned than others about the potential risks; some feel that the accomplishment of making an arms control agreement outweighs what they regard as largely illusory dangers. Some are concerned only with limited aspects of the negotiations, such as arrangements relating to the disposition of any troops the Soviets agree to withdraw from Central Europe. Some are better informed than others. Some are more active participants than others in force reduction matters.

In the business of force reduction proposals and negotiations, the United States, the United Kingdom, and the Federal Republic of Germany have been the Big Three. They are the participants with the greatest resources for study and analysis of the problems related to the undertaking. They are the participants with the largest defense budgets and military forces. The three nations have maintained a particularly close relationship in their work on MBFR matters.

In the early period of NATO's consideration of MBFR, the United Kingdom provided perhaps more motive power to the process than any other nation—particularly through its representative in the MBFR Working Group, Brigadier Richard Lloyd. The British, beset by economic strains and civil strife in Northern Ireland, have good reason for welcoming an opportunity to reduce their military forces on the continent of Europe. For the past thirty years, the British have been reducing their military commitments and shrinking the size of their military forces. Yet, despite the cutbacks, the United Kingdom still devotes to defense a greater share of its gross national product than does any other West European nation. During the last two decades, the British have reduced their military personnel by 40 percent, but they have largely spared their Army of the Rhine from the impact of defense cuts. London's desire for MBFR has been tempered by a high degree of caution. From the beginning, the representatives of the United Kingdom have played a restraining role with respect to MBFR, and they are particularly alert to the risks in any proposals that are considered.

From mid-1971 on, it has been the United States that has sup-

54

plied the leadership in NATO on force reduction negotiations. It has exercised the dominant influence on pace and timing of the actions of the alliance and has originated the bargaining proposals offered by the West. The tradition that NATO proposals are all made in Washington was broken in 1977 with the introduction of one made in Bonn, but even this proposal, in its finished form, bore some marks of American craftsmanship.

Domestic pressures within the United States to reduce American forces in Europe were important in moving NATO to seek force reduction talks. It was the strong support for reduction in the Senate that awakened the interest of the Nixon administration in MBFR. Congressional pressure for thinning out American troops in Europe first assumed serious proportions in 1966, and it persisted until 1974—except for a period of relaxation in 1968 following the Warsaw Pact invasion of Czechoslovakia.

In 1971, the Mansfield resolution calling for a 50 percent reduction in American forces in Europe was perceived by the Nixon administration as a serious threat to NATO's strength. Administration lobbying to defeat the Mansfield resolution received valuable, and perhaps decisive, support from Brezhnev, who five days before the Senate vote delivered a speech in Tiflis inviting the West to "taste the wine" of negotiation on force reductions in Europe. The resolution went down to defeat by a vote of 36 to 61.[5]

The United States at this time began to show a sense of urgency in moving forward NATO studies on MBFR negotiations. With Brezhnev beckoning on one side and Congress brandishing its meat ax on the other, prudence counseled moving toward the conference table to talk about mutual force reductions.

When the United States became serious about MBFR, its new attitude stirred others in the alliance to greater interest. This interest was stimulated in part by the fear that, if no negotiations took place, the United States would unilaterally reduce its forces in Europe. The more suspicious allies harbored the thought that Secretary Kissinger might negotiate a bilateral reduction agreement with the Soviet Union as part of some grand design, leaving Western Europe in a perilous position. For such reasons, the tactics of our allies with regard to force reduction negotiations have been designed throughout to ensure that they are not left out of the process.

---

[5] Senator Gaylord Nelson of Wisconsin, who voted against the Mansfield amendment, said "the Mansfield Amendment would have passed if Mr. Brezhnev had not said, 'we are willing to negotiate' and repeated it three times." *Congressional Record*, May 18, 1971, p. 15900.

The role of leadership the United States exercises among the NATO nations in force reduction negotiations follows from the fact that this country is the most powerful member of the alliance. Without the United States, there can be no credible deterrent to Soviet aggression and no firm basis for the political independence of Western Europe. The contribution of the United States to the NATO deterrent is not to be measured in terms of the military manpower this country stations in Europe; this amounts only to about 10 percent of the total NATO military forces. Nor can the United States' contribution be measured in terms of its numerically more impressive share— about 25 percent—of the Western ground forces located in Central Europe. The United States is the most important member of the alliance because it alone possesses significant strategic power, it provides the major share of the most modern and effective weaponry and equipment at NATO's disposal, and it has human and material resources greatly exceeding those of any other NATO nation. The 300,000 American military personnel based in Europe make an indispensable contribution to Western defense, and their presence signals to both sides of the iron curtain that the full military power of the United States would be employed if Western Europe were attacked. To some of our allies, any lesser American troop presence is a sign of weakening of Washington's commitment to the alliance. In intra-alliance negotiations on the Western force reduction position, this cast of mind manifested itself in efforts to impose special restrictions on the volume of the reduction of American troops.

The Federal Republic of Germany approached MBFR negotiations with some ambivalence. Chancellor Brandt's eagerness to maintain the momentum of détente after the 1970–1971 agreements with the East was counterbalanced by skepticism about the possibility of an agreement with the Soviet Union which would not impair West Germany's security.[6] As the NATO nation geographically closest to the Pact, as the major part of the reduction zone in the West, as the Western nation with the largest military force in Central Europe, and as the special object of Soviet hostility, West Germany has more at stake than any other participant.

An interesting evolution has taken place in the attitude of the

---

[6] The West German position at the opening of negotiations was summarized in ten points published under the heading "MBFR Policy of the Federal Government" in *The Security of the Federal Republic of Germany and the Development of Our Armed Forces: White Paper 1973–74* (Bonn: Defense Ministry, 1974). See also Walter F. Hahn, *Between Westpolitik and Eastpolitik: Changing West German Security Views* (Beverly Hills, Calif.: Sage Publications, 1975).

56

German government toward the negotiations. Having played earlier a largely reactive role toward the talks, the Germans in 1977 appeared to be leading the efforts to break the deadlock in Vienna with a new approach. In the course of the 1976 election campaign, Chancellor Schmidt, unlike campaigning politicians in other NATO countries, used MBFR as a talking point, calling himself "the father of MBFR," expressing dissatisfaction with the stalled negotiations, and asserting that political leaders should now step in to take the negotiations out of the hands of technicians. In the early summer of 1977, the German press indicated that a new approach was being formulated in Bonn, and in meetings with President Carter in Washington in July, Schmidt presented his suggestions to the U.S. government. This seems to be the first instance in the MBFR negotiations in which the lead in formulating Western proposals was taken, not by Washington, but by another member of the alliance.

West Germany appears to be the only NATO country in which MBFR has been the subject of recent spirited partisan debate. Willy Brandt, chairman of the Social Democratic party, and Herbert Wehner and Alfons Pawelczyk, party experts on foreign policy and disarmament, have been dropping hints since the early months of 1977 about the desirability of introducing a more flexible Western position into the negotiations and of meeting the East half way.

Pawelczyk, surveying the present status of the Vienna negotiations, concluded that "it is possible to reach concrete political results on the basis of what has been achieved so far." Putting aside the dispute about existing force levels on the two sides, he argued, an agreement could be concluded for a first-step reduction of American and Soviet forces, with a promise by all other direct participants in the negotiations to reduce their forces later. The reduction might be small, but that is unimportant. "The fact of reduction," Pawelczyk has said, "is of primary significance . . . rather than the volume of reduction in an initial agreement."[7]

Alois Mertes, the foreign policy spokesman for the Christian Democratic Union (CDU) and the Christian Social Union (CSU) members of the Bundestag, responded sharply to the hints and suggestions from the Social Democratic party spokesmen. He alleged that their remarks "can only enhance the East's adamant attitude so far displayed because they signal the chance of a softening of the Western negotiating position." When the decision was made to enter

---

[7] Alfons Pawelczyk, "Possibilities of a Reduction of Forces in Europe: Positions and Movements in the Vienna MBFR Talks," *Die Welt*, April 13, 1977.

the negotiations, Mertes said, the CDU/CSU "appreciated" the French arguments against MBFR. His party agreed to go along with "the highly problematic idea" only with the provisos that it lead to East-West parity and that the West refrain from engaging in any negotiation with the East on the Bundeswehr or on Western defense structure generally.[8]

Among the other Western nations, Belgium and the Netherlands exercise a marked influence. Both nations are within the reduction area, and consequently both have a reason for concern about the outcome. The influence they exercise, however, is perhaps due as much to the quality of their representatives as to other factors.

The principal interest of the countries that make up NATO's flanks —the indirect participants in the Vienna negotiations—is in avoiding an agreement that may increase the Soviet military presence close to their frontiers. They are concerned about provisions governing the disposition of the Russian forces that are withdrawn from Central Europe, and they hope to include in any agreement arrangements that will prevent circumvention. On other matters, the indirect participants —except for Italy—tend to defer to the direct participants in the negotiations.

Negotiation in Vienna

Once a week—every Thursday morning—when the Vienna negotiations are in session, the representatives of the nineteen NATO and Warsaw Pact nations assemble in the elegant gala hall of the Hofburg, where fancy balls were held at the time of the Congress of Vienna. This meeting is called a plenary, and it is the formal and official forum for the MBFR negotiations. At this meeting each side formally offers its proposals, and words spoken here take on an official and authoritative ring.

By the end of the thirteenth round of the negotiations on December 15, 1977, 157 plenary meetings had taken place, few of them enlivened by the submission of proposals and none by the sharp direct exchange of spontaneous debate. The plenary is structured, formalized, and stylized. Typically, a spokesman for one side reads a prepared paper; it is heard without comment; then the plenary adjourns until the following Thursday.

The plenary presumably gives the indirect participants a sense of

---

[8] Alois Mertes, "CDU Deputy Expounds Party Stance on Disarmament, MBFR," *Die Welt*, May 9, 1977.

58

involvement; it is the only meeting of the two sides to which indirect participants are regularly invited. It serves some public relations purpose in that it is always followed by a press conference at which spokesmen for East and West appear. But clearly it is not a forum for the give and take of negotiation.

Tuesday is the day on which representatives of the two sides meet in what are called "formal informals." The United States and the Soviet Union are always in attendance along with two other direct participants from each side on a rotating basis. These are high-level meetings, attended by the ambassadors. The business of these meetings is largely probing by each side—to seek explanation and clarification of each other's statements and positions, to accumulate the latest information, to detect any shift of position, to draw out what is really behind the rhetoric used in the plenaries and press releases.

A third type of negotiating forum, called the "informal informal," is in settings such as social gatherings, unrelated to the negotiations; these encounters are an important part of diplomatic life in a city noted for *gemütlichkeit*. It is in the informal meetings rather than in the plenaries that the real business of negotiating goes on.

For the Western representatives, there is another side to the proceedings in Vienna besides negotiating with the Warsaw Pact. Negotiations are also required among the NATO nations, particularly the direct participants, and Monday and Wednesday are the days for this. Staff members, who assemble at the beginning of each week, pool information secured from contact with the other side, with their national capitals, and with Brussels. They work on the statement that their spokesman will present at the next plenary. They assure common understanding of NATO positions—that the Western participants are moving in step toward the same objective at any given time.

The negotiators on the Western side in Vienna can not formulate policy. The negotiating positions they take are set in Brussels. They do, however, have considerable leeway in deciding on tactics and timing. Within the guidelines set by NATO, they exercise discretion about the content of statements and press releases and the general approach to the negotiating process.

The delegation of each Western nation maintains close contact with its own national capital. It is more likely to secure from that source than from Brussels advice about tactical questions and the handling of day-to-day problems. Conversely, a national delegation that desires some modification in NATO's instructions will be inclined to follow the indirect route of inspiring its national authorities to propose the change in NATO councils.

59

Perhaps the most significant attribute of the performance of the Western nations in the force reduction negotiations is the solidarity they have maintained from the beginning. Achieving a unified Western position on all the important issues that have been addressed during the course of the talks is remarkable.

The East's Negotiation Methods

Solidarity has also characterized the East's position in these negotiations, but this is less remarkable. The Warsaw Pact nations refuse formally to recognize the bilateral character of the negotiations, insisting that they are not "bloc-to-bloc" talks but that each nation is participating solely in its own individual capacity. This image does not fit the conduct of either Eastern or Western nations in Vienna.

Soviet disinterest in talking with NATO nations about force reductions in Central Europe was apparent long before the talks began. NATO's repeated invitations to open negotiations were ignored by Moscow, as were the vigorous efforts of NATO's explorer, Manlio Brosio, to arrange an audience at the Kremlin. The negotiations came about through bilateral dealings of the United States with the Soviet Union. Even after a date had been agreed on by the two major powers, the Warsaw Pact nations let two months go by before responding to the Western invitation to meet, and then they objected to the place and the guest list.

The preparatory talks, which began on January 31, 1973, with a brief opening meeting, promptly bogged down in haggling over such matters as inscriptions on the badges for delegates and the list of conference participants. The disputes went on for almost four months before a second formal meeting for preliminary negotiations could be held. The dilatory tactics of the East in this instance were designed apparently to avoid too close a temporal linkage of the force reduction talks with the Conference on Security and Cooperation in Europe, then under way in Helsinki.

Since the beginning of the negotiations proper, the Warsaw Pact has shown that it is in no hurry to reach an agreement. Although it submitted its original reduction proposal promptly, it has been slow to respond since that time. The best example of the Pact's tactics of delay and obstruction is its treatment of the question of the size of its forces in Central Europe. Clearly, meaningful negotiation on the East's reduction proposal depends on the head count of Pact forces in the reduction area. The Pact nations called for an equal percentage

60

reduction of forces in Central Europe, but they could hardly expect progress until they revealed their understanding of the base figure for Eastern forces to which the percentage would apply. Nevertheless, the East held back its figure for more than two and a half years after the negotiations opened.

The figure that the East submitted in June 1976 proved to be substantially below the Western estimate. Since mid-1976, the negotiations have been stalled in argument about the disparity between Eastern and Western figures. The East has argued that each side should accept the other's count of its own forces. The West has sought a breakdown of the East's figure as a step toward reconciliation of the disagreement. Finally, in late 1977, the Pact nations indicated they were ready to break their count down into categories proposed by the NATO side, but they attached to their offer the unacceptable condition that the West promise to ask no further questions about the Warsaw Pact troop count.

A possible explanation of the disparity between the two sides' count of Pact forces is lack of a common definition of ground manpower. This is not the root of the problem, however. If it were, the Communist states would not be resisting efforts to arrive at an agreement on definitions and analysis of the composition of Eastern forces. This resistance makes it impossible to credit the East with good faith in this dispute.

The Soviet Union uses the Vienna negotiations from time to time as a backdrop for propaganda, inveighing against the West for making qualitative improvements in its forces in Central Europe and for planning to introduce new generations of weapons. The Russians contend that such actions violate the spirit of the agreement to enter into force reduction negotiations. Currently, the Pact's protest is directed against any NATO move to introduce the neutron bomb or the cruise missile in Europe. The complaints of the East about NATO force improvements are transparent attempts to establish a double standard imposing restraints applicable only to the West. There is no sign of a slowdown in the considerable improvement in the firepower and the mobility of Soviet forces in the region.

What the Soviet Union would like to get out of the Vienna negotiations was summarized by Robert Legvold of the Russian Research Center of Harvard University as:

(1) establishing control over the evolution and growth of the Federal Republic's bundeswehr; (2) establishing a *droit de regard* over West European efforts at defense cooperation and integration; (3) influencing the nature and timing of

U.S. force withdrawals; and (4) attacking the forward-based-system (FBS) problem from another direction.[9]

Soviet proposals and Soviet rhetoric at Vienna are consistent with these objectives. Clearly, these goals will not be gained in the near term, but the East can afford to wait to see whether the Vienna negotiations will produce progress toward any of these objectives.

The Soviet Union is comfortable with the unhurried pace at Vienna and disinclined to take any initiative to break the logjam. It is probably a fair appraisal of the present strategy of the Warsaw Pact to say that the East will continue to mark time in the belief that it has not yet heard the best offer the West will make.

---

[9] "The Soviet Union and Current Multilateral Arms Negotiations," in Lawrence L. Whetten, ed., *The Future of Soviet Military Power* (New York: Crane Russak, 1976), p. 174.

4

The Future of the
Force Reduction Negotiations

The thirteenth round of the Vienna negotiations closed on December 15, 1977, in stalemate. The negotiators had been unable to agree even on a procedure for reaching agreement on how many soldiers the Warsaw Pact has in Central Europe. Because of this failure, representatives of the Western nations decided not to submit to the East a new offer that would have softened their previous proposal on withdrawal of Soviet armored forces.

Where do the negotiations go from here? Four broad options are open. The first is to break off the talks. It would not be unreasonable to conclude that, after more than four years of fruitless negotiation, the time has come to ring down the curtain on the Vienna negotiations. On the Western side, at least—and perhaps on both—there is reluctance to take this step, which might be interpreted as an unreasonable and indifferent attitude toward curbing arms competition. To some degree, public opinion pressures tie the representatives of the United States and of the Western European nations to the bargaining table at Vienna for as long as the Eastern representatives continue to show up. In addition to this consideration, there is still optimism, guarded and cautious, that prospects for an agreement will improve, and this feeling provides a positive reason for continuing the talks.[1]

A second option is to continue to negotiate on the established track, to argue about proposals already offered, and to seek to reconcile the conflict on Eastern troop strength. The West cannot afford

---

[1] President Carter, expressing his "hopes for 1978" to James Reston, indicated that he expected a SALT II agreement and a comprehensive test ban treaty, and he predicted "a real future on force reductions." "I think," he added, "that will be concluded in '78." *New York Times*, December 5, 1977.

to drop the effort to reach agreement on the Warsaw Pact troop count, which is essential to any substantial troop reduction agreement. Further discussion of the reduction offers made by the two sides is likely to be sterile. Each side has about exhausted all possible explanations of its own position and of its objections to the proposals of the other side.

A third option is to put forth a new force reduction proposal, either offering more to the East or demanding less of it. This is the course the West was ready to pursue in late 1977 until the collapse of the effort to move toward agreement on the troop count. Under this option, the subject matter of the negotiations remains the same—reductions of manpower, arms, and equipment. What changes is the price each side would pay in an agreement to reduce forces.

The fourth option is to shift the focus of the talks from reduction of manpower and equipment to other measures which could contribute to increased stability and security in Central Europe without involving reduction of forces.

Terminating the Negotiations

Several influences will continue to militate against ending the negotiations. There is always hope that the next round of talks—or the one after that—will bring the breakthrough that will lead to an agreement, and there is always fear that termination would produce adverse public reaction.

In addition, two byproducts of the Vienna talks reinforce the reluctance to abandon the negotiations. Continuing the talks serves the purposes of two groups with divergent concerns. The meetings in Vienna and the dialogue they entail can be viewed as serving the cause of détente. They improve each side's understanding of the other's point of view, they help to break down communication barriers between East and West, and they are a common school in which representatives of East and West learn together the highly complex problems of arms control. Secretary of Defense Harold Brown put it in these words: "Even in the absence of an agreement, the talks themselves are a valuable indicator of whether the Soviets are serious about reducing the possibility of military conflict in Europe and of what they mean by détente."[2]

Those who are concerned about NATO's military strength view

---

[2] "Tools to Keep the Peace," *Atlantic Community Quarterly*, vol. 15, no. 2 (Summer 1977), p. 170.

the talks as a way of preventing a possible erosion of Western defense. As long as the negotiations continue, most NATO nations are under pressure to maintain their defense effort in Europe, and force reductions, which might be put into effect if the talks ended, are staved off. In general, the NATO nations have taken seriously the pledge they first made at Reykjavik in 1968, and since then, whenever their foreign and defense ministers have assembled, they have repeated the pledge "that the overall military capability of NATO should not be reduced except as part of a pattern of mutual force reductions balanced in scope and timing." Although the pledge does not bar all force reductions by individual nations, it has had a strong restraining effect.

The government of the Netherlands, for example, has held off implementing a decision it made in 1974 to reduce its military personnel strength by 15 percent, explaining that "it is clear that unilateral reduction of the peace-time strength of the Netherlands Army would have serious political repercussions on the position of the allies at the MBFR negotiations, as well as on the success of these negotiations in general."[3] In the United States year after year, MBFR was used by the Nixon administration to counter proposed reductions in American forces in Europe. It was argued that MBFR negotiations were either in prospect or in progress and that a unilateral withdrawal of troops would offer as a gift a concession for which the Warsaw Pact might be ready to pay. This was the administration's chief argument in battles against successive Mansfield resolutions.[4]

Pressures to keep talking in Vienna may wane, but they are not likely to disappear. Nevertheless, it is highly possible the negotiations may end without an agreement. The basic conflict between Eastern and Western negotiating positions may make an acceptable agreement unreachable. In time, a prolonged stalemate may lead to recognition that further negotiation is pointless.

Further Force Reduction Proposals

The pattern of the negotiations since each side submitted its original proposals suggests that, if there are to be major new substantive proposals, they must be initiated by the West. The Warsaw Pact is in the

---

[3] Netherlands Ministry of Defence, *Our Very Existence at Stake: The Defence Policy in the Years 1974–1983* (The Hague, 1974).

[4] For example, Nixon letter to Senator Stennis, November 23, 1971, and Nixon letter to Senator Hugh Scott, September 20, 1973, both of which are contained in *Documents on Disarmament* compiled annually by the Arms Control and Disarmament Agency.

habit of reacting to Western proposals by presenting counterproposals, but it does not seem inclined to take the lead.

What further modifications of its position might the West consider offering in Vienna? A long list of possibilities might be compiled, but a few examples may illustrate the general direction some of them might take. One possibility is to address the two basic issues which separate the two sides—the issues the West labels parity and collectivity. A compromise might be sought in which the West would yield somewhat on manpower equality if, in return, the Warsaw Pact would abandon its insistence on individual national ceilings. For example, the proposal might combine (1) manpower reductions on both sides that would reduce, but not eliminate, the disparity NATO feels exists in ground forces and (2) the establishment of a collective, but not equal, ceiling on ground force levels after both sides have reduced their forces.

A reduction formula which, without achieving parity, would still reduce the imbalance in manpower between the two sides would seem to be in NATO's interest. The West might improve its situation if, for example, its forces were cut by 100,000 and those of the Warsaw Pact by 175,000, thus reducing by half the superiority in manpower NATO attributes to the Pact. Giving ground on this issue might be considered because the NATO nations probably regard the collective ceiling as more important than achieving absolute equality in manpower.

In practical terms, the issue of collective and individual national ceilings boils down to whether a ceiling will be imposed specifically on the armed forces of the Federal Republic of Germany. Here, the West can be expected to adhere to its position without yielding, because of the strategic geographical position of the Federal Republic of Germany and its place in alliance defense. If armed conflict between East and West should erupt in Europe, the Federal Republic is the probable battleground. This is where the decisive action would take place. Unlike the United States and the Soviet Union, the Federal Republic lies within the reduction area, and it maintains the largest and best equipped West European military force in Central Europe. It does not have the option of transferring elsewhere forces that it cuts in compliance with a reduction agreement and returning them to Central Europe in time of crisis. The forces it cuts are lost. If other Western nations fail to maintain forces at the ceilings permitted by a reduction agreement, and if these levels are considered necessary for minimum defensive needs, West Germany would not wish to be barred from making up the difference.

66

There is yet another important consideration inclining the NATO nations to hold fast in rejecting individual national ceilings under a force reduction agreement. National ceilings impair flexibility in choosing patterns of reorganization of future military forces, and they restrict types of reorganization that would integrate all or parts of the armed forces of several nations. National ceilings also limit the possibilities of introducing specialization by function in Western forces. Unity of Western Europe, political or military, is a distant goal, but the Western nations do not want to accept restraints that will be obstacles to achieving it.

A much more modest approach to compromise in the negotiations would be to set aside other issues and seek a simple agreement limited to a manpower reduction on both sides. The reduction that such an approach would produce would be largely symbolic, involving a relatively small number of troops and no commitment to further reduction. Such a step could be taken mutually even without formal agreement, or it could be taken unilaterally by one side in the hope that it would induce parallel action by the other side. Some observers believe that a unilateral gesture of this kind would be worth trying as a means of breaking the logjam. Those favoring a small, symbolic force reduction, whether mutual or unilateral, feel this step could create a psychological climate that will infuse new life into the negotiations and lead toward bolder measures.

This step has attendant risks, however. If a mutual symbolic reduction were agreed on, in all probability it would affect equal numbers of troops on both sides—a tacit acceptance of the Warsaw Pact theory of troop reduction and a potential impediment to any subsequent effort by the West to achieve "balanced" reductions. A unilateral Western reduction, designed to coax a response in kind from the East, might be taken as a signal that Western resolve is melting, thus encouraging the East to wait it out in anticipation of further unilateral concessions. Further, once a Western democratic nation has withdrawn a part of its forces from Central Europe, it may encounter serious political obstacles in trying to reverse course if the East fails to respond in kind. Nor does history provide much reason for anticipating that the Soviet Union would reciprocate a unilateral withdrawal of some American forces. As the accompanying graph suggests, changes in Soviet manpower levels in Europe are determined by factors other than the changes in the level of U.S. forces in the region.

Both sides have indicated that manpower levels are not their only major concern and have introduced other elements into their proposals. Compromise proposals that go beyond simple manpower reductions compound the difficulties of attaining agreement, however. It is hard to measure equivalency in dealing with arms and military equipment—how much "quid" equals a given amount of "quo." New efforts could be made to find an acceptable formula for trading off Soviet tanks against American tactical nuclear weapons. The West could ask less of the Pact than the withdrawal of an entire Soviet tank army including its 1,700 tanks and all equipment (as it was prepared to do in late 1977), or it could offer to remove more than 1,000 of its own tactical nuclear weapons with certain delivery systems.

Another possible approach is to add to the proposal offered for negotiation other types of armament and equipment regarded as particularly threatening. This could be in the form of removing arms now located in the reduction area or of pledging to limit or ban completely weapons systems not yet deployed. What turned out to be a

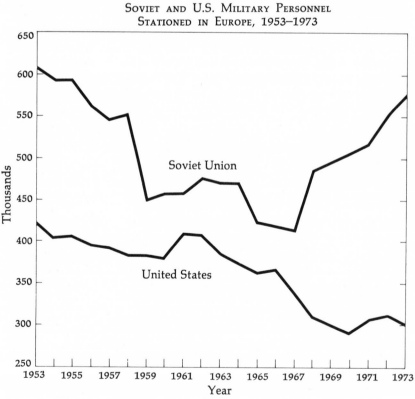

SOVIET AND U.S. MILITARY PERSONNEL
STATIONED IN EUROPE, 1953–1973

Source: Department of Defense; data are for the end of each calendar year.

68

false start in this direction was made within the U.S. government in November 1977, when a proposal to offer to the Warsaw Pact a pledge not to deploy neutron bombs in the reduction area was brought before the National Security Council. The National Security Council decided against the proposal. Subsequently the head of the Soviet delegation in Vienna, Nikolai Tarasov, indicated that if the offer had been made it would not have helped progress toward agreement.[5]

The conflict between East and West about the phasing of reductions can be bypassed by agreeing on a symbolic first-phase reduction and leaving subsequent reductions open for later discussion. The concept of phased withdrawals, beginning with American and Soviet forces in the first step, has been accepted by both sides, however, and both sides want, in connection with a first-phase agreement, some kind of commitment relating to subsequent reductions. The Western proposal asks for a first-phase agreement that guarantees no more than entry into negotiations on a second phase of reductions. There is something of the pig in a poke about this offer, and the West could afford to be more generous. The proposal could be modified either to accept the Eastern position, which in effect requires a single agreement covering Phase I reductions and the essentials of a Phase II reduction, or to reach an understanding at the time of a first agreement on general guidelines for a Phase II reduction. There is, of course, no reason why reductions could not be carried out in more than two phases if adding Phase III or Phase IV would help to surmount any problems blocking agreement. In any event, implementation of each phase could be dependent on the good faith execution of earlier phases. With a solution of the phasing issue, the issue of a freeze on manpower would evaporate. The West has declared itself ready to accept a freeze when an agreement for an initial phase of troop reduction has been concluded.

Any feasible compromise on the issue of arrangements for verification of agreed reductions will disappoint those who want strict measures to prevent cheating. This subject has not been prominent in the Vienna talks, but it is clear that there will be disagreement if this issue is ever reached. In informal conversations during the preliminary talks in Vienna, there was an East-West skirmish on the matter. According to the *New York Times*, the West at that time proposed verification procedures to establish the troop count and troop reductions under an agreement. The Russians, the report said, in-

---

[5] "Talks on European Troop Cuts Adjourn," *Washington Post*, December 16, 1977.

69

formed the Western powers that they would "object to verification in any part of Central Europe where they have troops."[6]

There is an ambivalence among representatives of NATO nations about the need for strict verification provisions in a force reduction agreement. Although the official NATO position inclines in that direction, many people believe that tight verification arrangements are either unnecessary or undesirable for the West. U.S. military sources express confidence in NATO's estimate of Warsaw Pact forces now in Central Europe, an estimate arrived at without such measures as stationing inspectors in Eastern Europe, and it is argued the same methods would be sufficient to detect cheating on any significant scale after the conclusion of a force reduction agreement. Bulwarking this position is the attitude of some Western nations which would not welcome Soviet inspection of their own territory.

In the bilateral agreements between the Soviet Union and the United States, such as SALT I and the agreement on nuclear testing, efforts by the United States to secure on-site inspection within Soviet territory have been unavailing. The pattern has been to rely on "national" means of verification to ensure compliance. This pattern will probably be followed in any force reduction agreement, but relying solely on national means of verification in the case of limiting manpower carries a larger measure of risk that violations of the agreement will not be promptly detected than it does in the case of limiting ICBMS or nuclear testing.[7]

Another issue related to the MBFR negotiations, that of circumvention, is of special concern to the nations of NATO's southern flank —Italy, Greece, and Turkey. It does not seem likely that the Soviet Union would accept any limitation on the number of troops it may station anywhere within its borders, and efforts to write into an agreement provisions to prevent a Soviet buildup adjacent to the Balkans or Turkey would be unproductive. It would be difficult to make a persuasive case for restrictions on the location of withdrawn forces within the Soviet Union, but transfer of such forces to Hungary would be a different matter. Western Hungary is closer to the Federal Republic of Germany than many parts of Poland. The question of

---

[6] "USSR Objects to West's Verification Proposals," *New York Times*, May 11, 1973.

[7] Jan M. Lodal, "Verifying SALT," *Foreign Policy*, no. 24 (Fall 1976), pp. 40–64. Lodal asserts that "relatively modest troop reductions such as those most commonly discussed for an MFBR first step cannot be verified with high confidence by 'national technical means.'" He seems to hold that reduction of large numbers, particularly of entire units, can be verified by such means.

70

whether Hungary is to be included in the reduction area is technically not finally settled, although the West has all but conceded on this issue. Nevertheless, before giving up the fight, the West could still seek as a quid pro quo for its concession a noncircumvention provision preventing the withdrawal of Soviet forces from the reduction area into Hungary. If an agreement is concluded at Vienna with little or nothing in the way of a noncircumvention provision, some difficulty may arise in securing the approval of the NATO council because of the disappointment of the countries that make up the southern flank. The flank countries have more of a voice in Brussels than they do in Vienna.

Associated Measures

The subject matter of the Vienna negotiations, as defined in the communiqué resulting from the preparatory talks, is "mutual reduction of forces and armaments and associated measures in Central Europe." The Warsaw Pact nations have tended to give a strict construction to the words "associated measures," arguing that any measures *not* associated with the mode of reduction are not within the purview of the negotiators. The subject has received little attention at Vienna, and, despite early negative reaction from the Warsaw Pact nations, opening it up for thorough discussion is an option the West could pursue. Such a discussion would be responsive to those who, like Senators Nunn and Bartlett, believe that the new Soviet threat lies in its capability for overwhelming attack on Western Europe from a standing start and that the Vienna negotiations should center on means of reducing this threat. This option, it is true, shifts the talks away from their original major purpose— force reduction. But there are other ways of approaching the general goal set for the Vienna negotiations, that of increased stability and security in Central Europe. If the danger of surprise attack could be lessened by agreeing on mutual constraints other than force reduction, this agreement could be worth making, if it is possible to do so.

The apparent fruitlessness of the quest for agreement on force reductions may impel the West to try something else at Vienna. Modest though it is, the success at Helsinki in 1975 in reaching agreement on confidence-building measures could suggest an alternative course. Proposals could be offered to test the willingness of the Warsaw Pact to add to the constraints on military activity which its members accepted in the agreement reached at the Helsinki Con-

71

ference on Security and Cooperation in Europe.[8] The final act of the conference contained a short list of confidence-building measures relating to notification of military maneuvers, exchange of military observers, and notification of military movements. The thirty-five nations which subscribed to the final act agreed to give prior notification (at least twenty-one days in advance) of major military maneuvers (involving more than 25,000 troops) conducted on European territory. The obligation which the Soviet Union undertook in this regard was somewhat diluted; it extends only to maneuvers conducted within 250 kilometers of Soviet borders with any other European state. This was the only real obligation in the field of confidence-building measures assumed by the signatories of the Helsinki final act. The document did, however, contain words of encouragement for such measures as prior notification of smaller maneuvers, prior notification of major military movements, exchange of observers at military maneuvers, and visits by military personnel across national lines.

Presidents Ford and Carter have reported to Congress that there has been satisfactory compliance with the confidence-building measures provided in the final act.[9] Prior notification of all major maneuvers apparently has been given. The NATO nations seem to have been more forthcoming and liberal than the Pact about notification of smaller exercises and invitations to military personnel of other countries to observe exercises. Neither side has chosen to give prior notification of any major movements of military personnel.

One possible line of negotiation in Vienna is in the direction of strengthening the quasi-commitments assumed by both NATO and Warsaw Pact countries under the Helsinki final act. This might include such proposals as extending the obligation to give prior notification of maneuvers so that it will apply to exercises involving fewer than 25,000 men and specifying that each alliance must include the other's military personnel among observers invited to its maneuvers. Possibly major movements of military units to locations within some given area close to the border between East and West could be subject to prior notification. The specific confidence-building

---

[8] U.S. Arms Control and Disarmament Agency, *Documents on Disarmament, 1975* (Washington, D.C. 1977), pp. 304 ff. for text of Helsinki final act.

[9] The presidential semiannual reports to the Commission on Security and Cooperation in Europe are published by the Committee on International Relations of the House of Representatives. So far, three have been issued: President Ford's report of December 1976, and President Carter's reports of June and December 1977.

72

measures referred to in the Helsinki document do not, of course, exhaust the possibilities. Confidence-building measures include any measures which grant an adversary access to information not normally revealed. Eisenhower's open skies proposal at Geneva in 1955 was such a measure, as was the Eden Plan proposal to station radar observation posts on either side of the iron curtain manned by personnel from the other side.

Disengagement measures are another possible topic of discussion at Vienna. Disengagement is another type of measure that tends to reduce the possibility of surprise attack, and many proposals of this nature were made in the 1950s and 1960s. Measures the Vienna negotiators could consider might include a completely demilitarized zone along the iron curtain extending for a limited distance into East and West Germany and Czechoslovakia. Other possibilities might be to exercise restraint in such a zone by refraining from placing certain kinds of offensive forces and weapons there, or by commiting the United States and the Soviet Union not to station their forces there, or by banning military maneuvers in the border area.

The difficulty with disengagement measures from the Western point of view is that they reduce the already limited land area in which the defense of Western Europe must be conducted in the event of an attack from the East. For example, the distance from the eastern to the western border of the Federal Republic of Germany at its narrowest point is less than 250 kilometers. If a wholly or partially demilitarized area is extensive enough in the East to serve as an obstacle to sudden attack without warning, an equal area on the Western side may preclude effective forward defense and leave little room for maneuver.

Afterthoughts

At the outset nobody really wanted the negotiations on force reductions in Central Europe. They were accepted by the Soviet Union as the price for securing a conference on European security, and they were entered into by the West as a means of forestalling unilateral troop reduction, particularly the withdrawal of substantial American forces from Europe.

With the passage of time, these negative reasons for the talks have lost their force. The Helsinki conference has done its work, accomplishing Soviet objectives in part but disappointing Moscow by highlighting questions of human rights. In the United States, the

73

pressure for withdrawing American forces from Europe has been replaced by mounting concern about the Soviet military buildup.

The talks go on, presumably because each side clings to the hope that it may derive some advantage from them. Yet, neither side has strong incentives to reach an agreement. The West offers terms which require the Soviet Union to give up advantages it now enjoys. The Russians are unlikely to make such a sacrifice. They are relatively satisfied with the present military balance in Central Europe, and they are outpacing the West in strengthening their forces. The East offers terms that will perpetuate its advantages. The West, believing the present balance to be at best precarious for its military forces, cannot be expected to accept a reduction formula that would make the status quo permanent or that might increase its disadvantage.

From the point of view of the Western nations, no agreement that may be negotiated in Vienna will bring any appreciable benefit in terms of security unless it reduces the capacity of the Soviet Union to launch a sudden surprise attack. To achieve this result, an agreement must go beyond simple manpower reductions and affect the weapons and equipment and disposition of Warsaw Pact forces. An agreement that would enhance Western security would have to be asymmetrical in its provisions in order to overcome the Soviet Union's geographical advantage over the United States, because of its proximity to Central Europe.

In all probability, the force reduction negotiations will continue for a long time. Prolonged negotiations may put the resoluteness of the Western nations to the test. It may become increasingly difficult for political leaders in democratic nations to go on negotiating without coming to any agreement. Impatience and the desire for "success" in negotiations with the Soviet Union can dull the sagacity and the prudence of leaders who must propitiate an electorate. This type of impatience seems to explain the eagerness of some American officials to offer at Vienna a pledge not to deploy the neutron weapon. This offer was suggested even before presidential study of the weapon's deployment was complete and before the attitude of Western European nations toward the introduction of the weapon was clear.

Even the most comprehensive force reduction agreement that could be anticipated will be quite limited in its effect on the overall military balance. Not only is it not likely to cut deeply into existing conventional forces in Central Europe, but also its effects outside this relatively small area would probably be negligible. It would not reach to the strategic arsenals of the superpowers. It probably would not inhibit the replacement of older arms and equipment by new and

74

more powerful weapons and other qualitative improvements in forces within Central Europe. It probably would not mean a reduction in defense budgets; new and more sophisticated systems will be ever more costly, and manpower reductions will not offset the increasing costs of such systems—particularly if added benefits are provided to the remaining men in uniform.

The fourteenth round of the MBFR negotiations ended with developments which should be noted. On April 19, 1978, the closing day of the round that a Western spokesman characterized as "important and eventful," the West made the offer to the Warsaw Pact which had been approved by NATO in December 1977 but withheld at that time. The proposal eases the Western demand for withdrawal of Soviet tank forces. Coupled with this is another change in the Western position in the form of an offer to provide some kind of commitment on the amount and timing of Phase II reductions at the time a Phase I reduction is agreed on. The West emphasized, however, that these offers are conditioned on attainment of agreement by the two sides on manpower data. On this factual issue, round fourteen apparently yielded agreement only on the mode of exchanging data. Whether this is significant progress remains to be seen.

Round fourteen produced at least some movement—the first in two years—in the negotiations. It is not clear, however, that it is movement in the direction of agreement on basic issues. Nor is there much evidence of give on the part of the Warsaw Pact. The Soviet response to the new Western offer was a noncommittal promise to examine it. The major part of the Soviet response dealt with President Carter's decision of April 7, 1978, to defer production of the neutron bomb. This, the Soviets complained, did not satisfy their demand for assurances that the bomb would not later enter the Western arsenal.

The record of the force reduction negotiations to date is not conducive to an optimistic view of the ultimate outcome. Yet the objective of some reduction in the density of military might assembled in the heart of Europe which could lessen a sense of danger and improve military security need not be relinquished. It is an idea whose time certainly has not yet come but may one day. If it does, historians may conclude that the Vienna negotiations served a useful purpose.

75

$$
\begin{array}{r}
3.80 \quad^{2} \\
15 \\
\hline
1700 \\
380 \\
\hline
55.00
\end{array}
$$